Straitjacket

How Overregulation Stifles Creativity and Innovation in Education

George Goens and Philip Streifer

ROWMAN & LITTLEFIELD EDUCATION

A division of
ROWMAN & LITTLEFIELD.
Lanham • Boulder • New York • Toronto • Plymouth, UK

Published by Rowman & Littlefield Education
A division of Rowman & Littlefield
4501 Forbes Boulevard, Suite 200, Lanham, Maryland 20706
www.rowman.com

10 Thornbury Road, Plymouth PL6 7PP, United Kingdom

Copyright © 2013 by George Goens and Philip Streifer

All rights reserved. No part of this book may be reproduced in any form or by any electronic or mechanical means, including information storage and retrieval systems, without written permission from the publisher, except by a reviewer who may quote passages in a review.

British Library Cataloguing in Publication Information Available

Library of Congress Cataloging-in-Publication Data

George Goens and Philip Streifer
  Straitjacket : how overregulation stifles creativity and innovation in education / by George Goens and Philip Streifer.
    p. cm.
  Includes bibliographical references.
    ISBN 978-1-4758-0563-5 (cloth) — ISBN 978-1-4758-0566-6 (paper) — ISBN 978-1-4758-0568-0 (electronic)
Public schools—Decentralization—United States. 3. School management and organization—United States. 4. Educational change—United States. I. Title.
  LC89.G63 2013
  379—dc23
                                                                    2010037457

Contents

Preface		v
1	Straitjacket	1
2	The Context for Schools and the Expanding Federal Role	7
3	The Narrowing Corridor: Why Deregulate?	21
4	The Growing Impact of Regulation on Public Schools	33
5	The Truth about Achievement and the Preparation Gap	43
6	Context, Complexity, and "Complicatedness"	69
7	Unshackling Creativity and Innovation	87
8	Culture Matters	99
9	So What Does This All Mean?	109
10	Eight Rules to Guide Real Reform of American Public Education	125
Appendix A: History of Federal Involvement in Education		145
Appendix B: Mandates—Bristol, CT, Public Schools		149
About the Authors		153

Preface

The expression often voiced among school staff that "reforms come and go—this too shall pass" is clichéd but true. As two former superintendents of schools, we've experienced this ourselves, given the myriad of national and state reforms over the years. We have also recognized that as we took on superintendencies our staffs often had the same initial view of our improvement initiatives for the district—so we are sensitive to how initiatives are often greeted. But as the years passed we noticed that national and state reforms were growing more and more politically driven, often not making educational sense. Worse, they sometimes had perverse effects on local districts, and schools and children.

We consider ourselves practitioner-researchers. We've held five superintendencies between us with a total combined twenty-nine years of experience in that top chair in both urban and suburban districts in several Midwestern and New England states. We have both also been full-time professors of educational administration at state-level and private universities. We've published several books on various related topics. In a nutshell, we are school leaders but also knowledgeable about the theoretical issues undergirding recent reforms and improvement strategies. Over the past thirty years, but particularly for the past decade or so, we have noticed the stifling of local discretion and decision making on just about every topic and issue facing schools today.

The time period from the late 1990s to the mid-2000s was particularly troubling as the No Child Left Behind Law (NCLB) had a major negative impact on schools. School curricula narrowed with a de-emphasis on the arts, science, and social studies because they were neither tested nor counted in the Adequate Yearly Progress Monitoring of NCLB. Local administrators became obsessed with "making AYP" rather than engaging in more thoughtful, longer-term improvement strategies.

State departments of education shifted from a helping to a monitoring and regulatory role. Worse, all of this activity was driven to meet standards on state mastery tests that, by virtue of the limits of their construction, had little or no real use for teachers to guide instruction. Test prep flourished, taking precious time away from instruction. Untold sums of human and fiscal resources were wasted on chasing test scores rather than in solving the real problems facing teachers and principals.

From this point of view one might think that we are just anti-test and anti-accountability programs. That is not the case, as we are actually well versed in the world of assessment literacy and psychometrics. We understand numbers, test scores, and accountability systems. What we've noticed, though, and what we've become concerned with, is the widespread misapplication of test metrics in ways that are just plain erroneous in many cases and that are having adverse effects on schools, teachers, and children.

The "straw that broke the camel's back" for us, and the reason we wrote this book, is the perverse way in which all of this politically driven reform, the misapplication of assessment and carrot-and-stick accountability has become the major driver of reform. Most recently this mind-set has schools focused on the use of student achievement test scores for evaluating teachers, which is a gross misapplication and use of these tests. We could not conceive of a more wrong way to bring about change and reform of public education to meet a changing context.

We have also seen how local administrators and teachers shy away from risk-taking and innovation, often concerned that a new direction or initiative might have a negative impact on students' scores, which could in turn cause them to lose their job. As a result, creativity and innovation are being stifled. Yet it is this very characteristic that we most need in our superintendents, teachers, and principals to solve the serious challenges posed by such diverse students in our schools.

Finally, we feel strongly that often voiced concerns about the achievement gap and how to address disparities in achievement between various racial, ethnic, and economic groups is seriously misplaced. Current national and state accountability plans often call for the closing of schools or other draconian measures such as replacing principals and teachers if achievement test score targets are not met. We know from the research literature, however, that the achievement gap in this country is in large part due to the preparation gap with which so many children enter school. Yet, far too few resources are being applied to that preparation gap; instead, we are now scapegoating teachers if students do not "measure up" to tests that they simply are unprepared by personal experiences to do well on.

At one point, about two years ago, we were talking over coffee about all of these issues, lamenting so much of the top-down control that is stifling local creativity and innovation in what we saw as a general downward spiral resulting in the formulation of more rules and regulations and a demoralized teacher and principal workforce. One thing we knew that we could do is to write this book as an "insider" view on what is really wrong with some schools and how to truly fix the problem. We also knew that not all schools are failing; in fact, many are doing extremely well, so we sought to set the record straight. Finally, we knew that a different direction is needed in national and state policy making so as to free up local teachers and principals to apply their creative energies to address the problems they face each day in the classroom.

We think this book provides a realistic perspective on these issues and recognizes the complexity of truly educating children. We have tried to limit the typical jargon that might come with a book about educational reform and improvement. We have also tried to tell it straight, neither mincing words nor shying away from focusing attention on the real problems of education today.

We also hope that this book brings hope to many that otherwise feel that their schools are failing—they are not in most cases. The straitjacket of centralized control and coercive approaches to the problems that public education is facing is not the solution, but actually is part of the problem. And where achievement is lower than desired we hope that this book brings attention to the root cause—lack of student preparation so that more resources can be put into catching these kids up, rather than into more tests, more curriculum development, and more administrative staff needed to comply with all of this complexity and growing regulations.

We are coauthors in this endeavor, listed in alphabetical order, sharing each view expressed throughout the book. Achieving that level agreement across so many complex issues took time and a great deal of effort, but we both stand behind each statement and opinion.

George A. Goens and Phil Streifer
May 2013

Chapter One

Straitjacket

Straitjackets were invented in France in 1790 at a time when mental health was a mystery. Doctors did not know how to treat mental disorders and they could not understand what caused the behavior of patients. So straitjackets were used in the belief that their patients were undisciplined—not in control of their behavior and needing an external restraint to get self-control. Patients needed to be constrained from physically hurting themselves or others. Straitjackets were used until psychoanalysis and psychiatric medications came into use, and research and knowledge about mental heath became more sophisticated.

While straitjackets are not used much today, they do exist in the metaphorical sense in organizations and leadership. The irony, however, is that this straitjacket can restrain the positive behavior of creativity and innovation: just as they were meant to restrain mental patients in the past, today the metaphorical straitjacket confines, restricts, or hinders the freedom of action, development, or expression in organizations, including schools.

These straitjackets severely limit generating imaginative approaches to problems, ideas, and actions in a way that is damaging to the long-term interests and adaptability of organizations. Innovation cannot occur if there are restrictions, constraints, impediments, hindrances, obstacles, barriers, encumbrances, obstructions, checks, and curbs placed on the ability of employees to manage their behavior.

Several types of straitjackets are at work today. Obviously, the physical straitjacket harkens back to a time of ignorance about mental health. However, there are two other straitjackets in play affecting individuals and organizations.

A major straitjacket is cognitive in nature. We get trapped in the confines of accepted thought or "group think." The cliché "thinking outside the box" illustrates that we can get confined to a set of accepted ideas, whether they are correct and effective or not. We tie ourselves down with conventional wisdom; the flavor-of-the-day ideas, many of which are unproven; or speculative proposals promoted by the media or prominent so-called experts or reformers. Too often, critical thinking is absent when examining ideas and initiatives proposed for public schools, and school leaders succumb to these jargonized slogans and initiatives.

Supreme Court Justice Antonin Scalia[1] indicated that lawyers and others must be able to make the case for their position, and one way to do that is to understand and be able to make the opposition's case. Educators need to do the same thing. Only then will we break out of the straitjacket, create a dialogue, and analyze, evaluate, and synthesize the value of ideas and initiatives. This means open discourse about what is potentially right and wrong about various reform initiatives by all involved. But that rarely happens in schools today, as teachers and principals find themselves in a compliance-driven organization.

Second, psychological straitjackets inhibit the ability to act. Some people and organizations collectively fall into the trap of believing that they cannot do it—that they lack the knowledge, skill, talent, or potential to solve their own problems. They believe that they must rely on so-called experts or people up the "food chain"—the state or federal government agencies and the bureaucrats within them. They succumb to the role of victim, a helpless mentality, feeling they don't have the knowledge, ability, or prerogative to find solutions and act. Passivity and victimhood are destructive and debilitating to the individual and to organizations. In doing so, they willingly surrender their discretion and prerogatives to make decisions that are most appropriate at the local level.

Leadership is a different matter. Some regard it as taking heroic action and saving the day from external threats or from internal ineptness of workers. To others, leadership is cracking heads and firing people to get the job done. In this model individuals are expendable. The "commanders" desire conformity and compliance to traditional and expected thought, placing a straitjacket on diverse or collective thinking within the organization. For others, and in our view, the role of the leader is to build the talent capacity within the organization to collaboratively find solutions and new approaches. The leader's primary role it to free individuals within the organization to unleash their inherent creativity and innovative energies to solve complex problems.

The straitjacket of traditional thought caused Kodak[2] to fall from a *Fortune* 500 company to a bankrupt former corporate giant. In the late 1980s and the ensuing decades, Kodak missed becoming a major force in the digital revolution, even though they were the first ones to create a digital camera. Inflexibility and failure or fear to adapt to changing times strangled the company.

They failed to transform and were stuck in an old paradigm, and old habits and regulations became obstacles to growth and continued success.

Public schools have been placed in a straitjacket, buckle by buckle, over the past thirty years or so through the growing power of the federal government over public education, enabled through federal regulation, court decisions, state government legislation, school board policies and procedures, and the media's influence on public opinion. In some instances a court ruling over a specific case or a piece of legislation over an isolated issue has impact throughout the nation or state.

Other cases, either through federal or state legislative action, legislative mandates, or their regulatory guidelines for implementation, have had a big effect on the discretion of local school districts and professionals. Some of this legislation has been proposed by special interests and are the product of the political legislative process and influence. An obvious historical example is collective bargaining with public employee groups that resulted in stipulated policies and procedures, and limited discretion on both teachers and school boards. Recently, "No Child Left Behind" greatly directed the educational programs and accountability procedures of school districts across the country, even though it had serious flaws and its primary goal was not feasibly attainable.

In the current context, the federal Department of Education and the Obama administration have used a coercive approach of "carrots and sticks" as their primary lever for change. For example, if states are interested in the "Race to the Top" grants, they have to legislate reforms prescribed by the federal model. In this model teacher evaluations must be designed around a particular approach using short-term, narrow student test results that in many cases have little or no connection to a particular teacher's work! Local innovation and creativity take a backseat to federal proposals and the desire of states to develop and present proposals around the federal paradigm. And of course, states strapped for cash due to the Great Recession wanted the money.

In a curious way, the straitjacket of mandates and regulations indicates a lack of confidence in local institutions, parents, teachers, principals, and superintendents to get the job done—to find solutions to educational issues. Consequently, there has been an increase in mandates and top-down rules and preferred practices and approaches to curriculum, instruction, assessment, and accountability. This drive to improve is motivated by a common belief that schools are failing and that there is a wide achievement gap that schools have been unable to address. However, we now know that the achievement gap is largely a result of the preparation gap that schools have few funds to address directly. Further we know that many schools are actually performing very well, given all their constraints. So the idea that schools need further restraints—or straitjacketing—is just not supported by the facts.

At the local level, schools are constrained by the straitjacket of "group think" that often leads to inaction because they believe that they do not have the prerogative or knowledge to act on their own. This emanates from the shackles of these mental models, paradigms, and critical assumptions that are advocated by reformers, legislators, and pundits. These cognitive templates include the following concepts:

- Everything that is of value is metrically measurable: education is synonymous with or equals passing student achievement tests.
- Technology is the prime answer to the problems in education.
- Schools are businesses and the market should drive them.
- "Carrots and sticks" and hierarchical power drive change.
- Centralized federal control is the answer to bringing about change at the local level.
- National standards will result in higher achievement and consistent outcomes.
- Accountability for schools rests on narrow achievement tests and the resulting scores.
- Education is a competitive race between individuals and countries based on test results.
- Education is simply a cognitive exercise that is separate from social, emotional, or cultural behavior.
- Leadership is power over people and its will is forced through hierarchical control.

These assumptions place a straitjacket on the nature and scope of the possible ideas to improve public education, how people think about them, and what action they take. Educators fall into the trap of conventional thinking based on these models, which stymies innovation in public education at the local level. Eventually, it can kill it—as what happened to Kodak. The following chapters will go into specific detail on how educators get tied into the straitjacket, the implications of the restraints, and the issues and approaches that can renew public education and improve the educational opportunities of children.

Politicians have pushed for many of these reforms and are largely responsible for the tightening straitjacket on schools. Ken Robinson defines the issue:

> All over the world, governments are pouring vast resources into education reform. In the process, policy makers typically narrow the curriculum to emphasize a small group of subjects, tie schools up in culture of standardized testing and limit discretion of educators to make professional judgments about how and what to teach. These reforms are typically stifling the very skills and qualities

that are essential to meet the challenges we face: creativity, cultural understanding, communication, collaboration, and problem solving.[3]

We live in a time of uncertainty, yet we often find ourselves in the straitjacket of hackneyed ideas and paradigms. We lose our curiosity or fall back and embrace older conventional ideas and approaches. We stop asking questions and look to others for solutions.

There is no Superman who will save our children (in reference to the movie *Waiting for Superman*). There are no magic bullets that can solve those problems that do exist, and there are no simple solutions or single causes of the problems we face. Special interests are not synonymous with the common good. Parents, teachers, administrators, and local school boards have a natural vested interest to work together to meet the needs of their children. Public education has been the bulwark of developing the creative and innovative genius of our children that has kept the United States the most prominent nation on the face of the planet. That is a sacred obligation we cannot hand off to for-profit enterprises, corporate market-driven organizations, or contemporary fads.

NOTES

1. Antonin Scalia and Brian A. Gardner, *Making Your Case* (St. Paul, MN: Thomas/West Publishers, 2008).

2. Tom Ahonen, "The Fall of Kodak: Lessons Learned," www.brightside.com, 2009.

3. Ken Robinson, *Out of Our Minds: Learning to Be Creative* (New York: Wiley, 2011), 14–15.

Chapter Two

The Context for Schools and the Expanding Federal Role

American public education carries the hopes of parents and the nation on its shoulders. Overall, it has been largely successful amid great social, technological, and political change over the past century. The American dream, based on opportunity, was dependent in large part on access to education. In America, education was not just for the elites, but also for all citizens. Education and opportunity were almost synonymous.

From the beginning of the twentieth century until its end, public education became available to all children including access to collegiate opportunities. In trying to fulfill its mission schools had to deal with huge social, economic, and global changes. However, schools and teachers did not have the ability to affect some factors that had a great influence on children, families, and communities. Too often schools were blamed for the challenges and issues we faced as a society. Some believe that schools should be the instrument for social change, political change, economic change, and technological change. Education became the generic answer to every problem or malady facing the nation.

But schools cannot be successful in isolation of parents and community. Diane Ravitch cites that parents "withdrew" from their responsibilities because of economic or other issues, resulting in children having greater liberty to do as they please.[1] In schools, disciplining children came under pressure because of litigation, community fragmentation, and the media's influence on children and society. Thus, acting "in loco parentis" (or "in place of parents") became more difficult for the schools. Family cohesion and structure, and a more permissive social structure affected children's attitudes, behavior, and respect for educators and teachers.

Over the past thirty years, the authority of principals and teachers greatly diminished. The impact of court decisions, and federal and state regulations and mandates grew. In fact, principals' and superintendents' focus became more tightly centered on negotiations, budgets, strategic plans, politics, metrics, and compliance with regulations than on curriculum and instruction over this time period.

While schools alone could not alter or rebuild society, they became larger and more complex than earlier in the century. Bureaucracy expanded as consolidation occurred based on efficiency of scale and operational philosophy. Large schools, particularly in urban areas, became less personalized. Schools were consolidated and increased in size under the guise of providing more comprehensive educational opportunities for children, as well as operating with greater financial and operational efficiency.

Education has always endured philosophical discussion and debate. Throughout the last hundred years, these debates along with associated movements, pushed for particular programs, initiatives, and outcomes for public schools. Some of these movements, including some today, are contrary to research and appropriateness for children. While data-based decisions are espoused, some of these initiatives (especially those tied to very narrow achievement tests where the inferences drawn are inappropriate—see chapter 5) are contrary to organizational and educational research based on findings from legitimate and long-standing studies and research.

The past century brought a potpourri of movements that tried to drive education in a particular direction for a specific purpose. Schools, according to Ravitch, were pushed to focus on "job training, social planning, political reform, social sorting, personality adjustment, and social efficiency."[2] The focal points for these movements include the 1960s with its concentration on relevance, the 1970s with its goal of minimum competency, and the 1980s and '90s with graduation requirements and higher expectations as the focus. And as the economy was threatened by international competition and began to sag, education was blamed for not providing skilled workers and educating them to be trained for new jobs.

Over the years public schools have faced initiatives, many of which were sound, that have come and gone, inspiring great pessimism on the part of teachers and principals. The list includes: constructivism, outcome-based education, standards-based education, experiential education, blended learning, school-to-work education, digital education, project-based learning, inquiry-based learning, multiple intelligence programs, and others. Most of the proposed reforms over the years emphasize the "hows" of instruction to achieve certain outcomes. Few concern the issues of the definition of an educated person directly—the "why" of education. This is no small issue, because it gets at the very core of what school reform should be focused upon.

For parents, a quality education has always been the essential backbone for their children's future. Going back to agrarian times through the Industrial

Revolution and to the present day, parents have understood that their child's future rests at the schoolhouse door. Parents, in essence, shop for a home in the best school system with the best educational opportunities they can afford.

Local municipalities, if they have any sense of their future prosperity, understand that the perception of their community rests primarily on the attractiveness of the public schools. Local communities compete primarily through their school districts, because they know their property values and the vibrancy of their town rests on the performance and opportunity provided by the public schools. The quality of schools is an issue locally and nationally.

The national dialogue on school reform has been swirling about for the past thirty years. The good news is that education is perceived to be a priority in the United States—no debate there. However, the quality of public schools and the way to improve them are in great dispute and controversy. The extent and reach of regulation and mandates are also major issues because they inhibit innovation and creativity that are essential for schools to adjust to changing conditions and times. How to nurture quality and creativity in schools must become part of the debate.

Education, until fairly recently, has been solely the province of state government. A big piece of the state budget and taxes go for public education. Each state has a bureaucracy in place to govern and regulate their school districts. Astute state politicians recognize that their economic development and welfare rest, in part, on the strength of their school systems. Corporations, businesses, and industries will not move into a state that cannot provide a workforce educated enough to be trained in today's technological and complex workplaces.

At the national level, the debate has focused on the fact that our economic and social conditions rest upon an educated citizenry. This has always been the case and always will be. The globalization of the economy, along with the realization that innovation is essential for the United States to thrive economically and socially, has underscored this reality. And our nation's schools have been recognized for developing intelligent, insightful, and creative entrepreneurs.

Thomas Jefferson's assertion about the necessity for an educated citizenry to maintain a democracy has always been a founding principle of American public schools. In addition, many see the United States as a country of "exceptionalism." Historically, whether with Western expansion or in contemporary times with international competition, we perceive ourselves as having the power to harness individual creativity and entrepreneurship to maintain and enhance our fiscal and social prominence. The American "can-do" attitude has rested on the originality, inventiveness, and adaptability of individuals who find answers and have the independent latitude to address issues in inventive ways. We have always prized our individualism and inventiveness.

Public education has been and always will be the cornerstone of our democracy and society. Over the decades it has educated immigrants from around the world, provided a strong cadre of creative individuals, and been the primary fuel for our economic growth and standard of living. In an ever more complex world today, public schools do not need a straitjacket, but need to be released and liberated from control-centric regulations, rules, and mandates that restrict the development of talent.

FEAR AND THE FEDS

The federal expansion into educational policy and programs in many respects is driven by fear and ignorance on the part of the public. The Sputnik era was pushed by fear that the Soviet Union was charging ahead in science and mathematics and beating us in the space race, as well as by our concern for containing the Russians' international role.

Sounds eerily familiar to contemporary times starting in the 1980s when the report *A Nation at Risk* was published, doesn't it? It is now alleged that public education is in crisis over the economic, political, and global standing of the United States. The perspective that public education here cannot match the systems overseas is widespread as our schools are accused of underperforming globally. These accusations have been based on "myth" created by selective data that have permeated politics and the media. According to Berliner and Biddle the crisis called "A Nation at Risk" was contrived and based on myths and deception.[3] And, a National School Board Association report, "Myths and Realities in Public Education," specifically cites inaccuracies and "cherry picked" data in these discussions.[4]

The federal government, it seems, achieves more bipartisan support if national security or safety is perceived to be at stake. From Sputnik to *A Nation at Risk* to the recent initiative called "Race to the Top," public schools and teachers have been criticized as jeopardizing our society; they are the reason for our business and industries not being competitive, the cause of civil strife and increasing social fragmentation. They are painted as the purveyor of mediocrity and ineffectiveness in addressing a broad range of educational, social, economic, and individual concerns, even though they do not have the power to do so. Schools have also been painted as resistant to change and locked in bureaucratic rigidity and union dogma.

Regardless of the facts highlighted by Berliner and Biddle, and others, a national movement to increase the role of the federal government in education gained momentum. Reforms have been structured so that organizations can offer to run schools as businesses, including the corporatization of education in the hands of nonprofit, for-profit, or other private alternatives to the public schools. Accountability, particularly based on test metrics, has been instituted at the federal level and "market-driven" solutions to solving "achievement gaps" through choice and other interventions have proliferated. However, very few of these reforms have focused on the root cause of poor student achievement where it exists—the preparation gap.

This debate about education, especially recently, has been filled with test statistics and other metrics; conflicting research findings; selective data; questionable conclusions; "magic bullet" solutions; and vested political, corporate, and foundation interests. In addition, the partisan political positions of conservatives and liberals about the role of education and what should be taught, how it should be taught, and how it should be assessed is debated in the media and in the electoral process. To local citizens, this debate can be confusing, tiring, alarmist and sometimes frightening.

THE IMPACT OF THE FEDERAL DEPARTMENT OF EDUCATION

In 1979 the Federal Department of Education was established and became a cabinet-level position. This was not without controversy, however, with significant debate and tight votes in the Congress. Appendix A summarizes the history of federal involvement in local education. The history from 1785 to the present illustrates that increasing federal control of education occurred through erosion over time in which states gave up their discretion in favor of compensation, or through fear, whether economic or international.

Released in June 2005, the U.S. Department of Education document, "10 Facts About K-12 Education Funding,"[5] supported the principle of helping states to establish effective schools. The first fact was that "the U.S. Constitution leaves the responsibility for public K-12 education with the states. The responsibility for K-12 education rests with the states under the Constitution. There is also a compelling national interest in the quality of the nation's public schools. Therefore, the federal government, through the legislative process, provides *assistance to the states and schools in an effort to supplement, not supplant, state support*" (our emphasis). Today, however, the federal role has morphed into burdensome mandates, regulations, and fiscal coercion that affect finances, programs, and accountability. Thus, the reality of a growing federal influence is in conflict with this "fact" as noted by the U.S. Department of Education. In order for this to have happened, states had to cede their influence and role.

The increasing federal role in education occurred by degrees, since 1867 when the original department of education was created to *collect information* on schools and teachers to help states establish effective school systems. Over the next 130 years, legislation regarding specific education issues and interests was fairly passive.

When education was moved out of the Department of Health Education and Welfare into the new Department of Education and became a cabinet-level agency in 1980, it was charged with creating a dialogue to improve the system through research, emphasizing the "twin goals of access and excellence" at every educational level. The mission of the Department of Education as stated on its website in 2010 is to "promote student achievement in preparation for global competitiveness by fostering educational excellence and ensuring equal access."[6]

Debate was vociferous about a cabinet-level education department. Backers of the idea thought it would lead to greater efficiency and more accountability, improve program management, and make federal assistance more responsive to state needs.

Opponents argued that the federal department would encroach on the state responsibility, establish a bureaucracy without assurance that there would be an improvement in education, and make things more complicated. Others were concerned that having a separate Department of Education would destroy the education–health–labor–civil rights department's cohesive impact over social legislation.

Still other resistance to the new department was based on the constitutional argument that the founders were correct to reserve education as a function of the state and local levels because it is the best way to protect individual freedom and develop and maintain a civil society based on limited and divided power. Each state would be able to innovate and have those innovations copied by other states without having one federal policy mandated from the top.

The Department of Education today touches every area and level of education. The emphasis of the federal government changed in the 1980s with priority placed on standards and accountability, which was a response to the perceived decline in education with the report *A Nation at Risk.*[7]

In 1983 *A Nation at Risk: The Imperative for Educational Reform*, a report from Ronald Reagan's National Commission on Excellence in Education was considered a landmark, even though a heartily refuted event in modern American educational history. Secretary of Education Terrel Bell stated that the United States' educational system was failing to meet the national need for a competitive workforce. The report stated: "the educational foundations of our society are presently being eroded by a rising tide of mediocrity that threatens our very future as a Nation and a people" and "If an unfriendly foreign power had attempted to impose on America the mediocre educational performance that exists today, we might well have viewed it as an act of war." This landmark report focused on achievement scores, graduation rates, student expectations, and academics. In addition, the charter school movement started in 1985 and carries on today with more states passing legislation enabling charter schools or increasing their numbers.

The ongoing concern for education nationally was a bipartisan movement that included Republican and Democratic presidents. In the 1994 Educate America Act: Goals 2000 the Clinton administration called for increased parental involvement, professional development for teachers, and support to states to develop standards and assessments. In addition, the reauthorization of ESEA (Elementary and Secondary Act) Improving America's Schools Act, Title I was revised to require economically disadvantaged students and others to be assessed against the same standards across the country. Schools with low performance were to be identified and provided extra assistance because they were in need of improvement.

The first decade of the twenty-first century began with the passage of the No Child Left Behind Act in 2001, enacted with bipartisan support, which required *all* students to be proficient in reading, mathematics, and science by 2014, with annual yearly progress (AYP) measures to determine success through annual standardized tests in grades three to eight in reading and mathematics. Sanctions were placed on schools not meeting AYP requirements, along with plans to close achievement gaps. This approach signaled a significant shift in strategy by the Feds from supporting programs for disadvantaged youngsters to specific direction and mandates from the federal government for curriculum, instruction, assessment, and accountability.

Since its inception in 2001, the federal government's role and influence has expanded and became a dominating force driven by No Child Left Behind (NCLB). In fact, Senator Carl Levin stated that the Bush administration turned No Child Left Behind Act into "yet one more unfunded mandate" pushed onto state and local governments.[8] This legislation imposed standards-based education reform and measurable test-based goals to improve individual outcomes in education. NCLB required states to develop assessments in basic skills to be given to all students in certain grades in order to receive federal funding.

IMPACT OF TEST-DRIVEN ACCOUNTABILITY

The power of test-driven accountability under NCLB has altered curriculum, instruction, and assessment. To bureaucrats in Washington, children have been reduced to mere metrics. Senator Leahy of Vermont criticized this, saying that a "one size fits all" approach has not worked for Vermont students and that he supports the reform of his state's current testing system.[9]

Former senator Russ Feingold of Wisconsin said in his September 1, 2010, newsletter, "One of the main reasons I voted against NCLB in 2001 was because Wisconsinites were concerned about the way the law focuses so heavily on testing and was inflexible when it came to the needs of local school districts."[10] Feingold was one of ten senators who opposed NCLB because of its annual testing and the fact that it posed a large unfunded mandate on states.[11]

The hand of federal control works in classrooms across the country every day as teachers "teach to the test" and as school boards narrow the curriculum focus and emphasize test metrics to the exclusion of other accountability methods. In doing so, creative teachers become frustrated, and inventive and critical thinking are minimized as educational goals. As a result, we are in danger of "well-schooling" but "poorly educating" children.

Accountability is important, but accountability for constitutional responsibilities should rest with the level of government designated in the national and state constitutions. Senator Leahy advocated for local control and flexibility. He said, "States need flexibility to design accountability measures that accurately reflect actual conditions and unique characteristics in real communities."[12]

Local and state school officials have a direct self-interest to design accountability systems that make sense and move beyond the simplistic metric of "high stakes" testing. After all, good schools are economic magnets that have an impact on housing, business, and jobs, as well as the quality of community life. In addition, the impact of teachers and schools may not be seen in the short-term. The impact of a great teacher may not be felt immediately or even over the course of the school year. Sometimes a teacher's impact is understood only in retrospect and in the reflection of time. Significance is not measured by a value-added analysis or by an evaluator viewing classroom practices or lesson plans a few times a year.

Accountability, evaluating teachers, and measuring "significance" is not easy to accomplish. We try to make it objective by throwing numbers at it via test scores. But none of us are the sum total of our tenth-grade standardized test results! Great teachers have impact beyond their "doings" of implementing best practices. It is their "being"—their character, disposition, essence, uniqueness, and integrity—that make them significant.

We forget that it is far, far easier to teach skills of lesson implementation. Heart and passion come from a different place. Authenticity and genuineness is not simply a cognitive process. Understanding how to work with children and others in a way that helps them fulfill themselves and find meaning, purpose, and a sense of wisdom cannot be reduced to simplistic processes, measurement, and metrics.

We all have experienced significant teachers who understood both the art and science of teaching and building constructive and compassionate relationships. And we are all thankful for those relationships and influences. None of us would be where we are without those teachers. We shouldn't forget that.

RACING TO THE TOP

In 2009 President Barack Obama stated on July 24, in announcing the "Race to the Top" program:

> America will not succeed in the 21st century unless we do a far better job of educating our sons and daughters. . . . And the race starts today. I am issuing a challenge to our nation's governors and school boards, principals and teachers, businesses and non-profits, parents and students: if you set and enforce rigorous and challenging standards and assessments; if you put outstanding teachers at the front of the classroom; if you turn around failing schools—your state can win a Race to the Top grant that will not only help students outcompete workers around the world, but let them fulfill their God-given potential."[13]

According to the White House the "Race to the Top" was designed to spur systemic reform and embrace innovative approaches to teaching and learning in America's schools. Backed by a historic $4.35 billion investment, the reforms contained in the Race to the Top program are supposed to help "prepare America's students to graduate ready for college and career, and enable them to out-compete any worker, anywhere in the world."

The major components of the "Race" included:

- *Designing and implementing rigorous standards and high-quality assessments,* by encouraging states to work jointly toward a system of common academic standards that builds toward college and career readiness, and that includes improved assessments designed to measure critical knowledge and higher-order thinking skills.
- *Attracting and keeping great teachers and leaders in America's classrooms,* by expanding effective support to teachers and principals; reforming and improving teacher preparation; revising teacher evaluation, compensation, and retention policies to encourage and reward effectiveness; and working to ensure that our most talented teachers are placed in the schools and subjects where they are needed the most.

- *Supporting data systems that inform decisions and improve instruction*, by fully implementing a statewide longitudinal data system, assessing and using data to drive instruction, and making data more accessible to key stakeholders.
- *Using innovation and effective approaches to turn around struggling schools*, by asking states to prioritize and transform persistently low-performing schools.
- *Demonstrating and sustaining education reform*, by promoting collaborations between business leaders, educators, and other stakeholders to raise student achievement and close achievement gaps, and by expanding support for high-performing public charter schools, reinvigorating math and science education, and promoting other conditions favorable to innovation and reform.

The list of goals is a far cry from the original department established in 1867 to collect information and help states establish effective school systems. The Race to the Top covers the major core of school operations. Examine the list from standards, to goals to assessments to teacher preparation to accountability, to data systems for instruction, to innovation, to charters, partnerships and STEM (science, technology, engineering and mathematics). This litany doesn't leave much to state departments except to be the bureaucratic broker for "Race" funding. The bottom line is a comprehensive strategy to reform education through a coercive fiscal carrot and reduced discretion at the state and local level.

Thus, while the federal Department of Education indicates that K-12 education is the right of the states under the Constitution in one statement, the federal government uses fiscal carrots and sticks in order to get state and local education agencies to comply through its incentives and sanctions during the second-worst national economic crisis of our lives.

With states being stretched financially and the cry from homeowners about the weight of property and state taxes that mostly fund public schools, few states or local districts are willing to reject federal funds. In addition, some of the mandates and programs prescribed by the Feds and the states are not fully funded at the local level, which amounts to "trickle down taxation" because while local districts are mandated to provide the program, neither the states nor the federal government provide sufficient funds to institute them fully, thereby having a direct impact on local taxes.

SUMMARY

The policy shift by the federal government in prescribing specific results has produced more direct control over educational policy at the state and local levels through legislation, regulations, and financial incentives or penalties. As a result, this centralized control often stymies local initiative, and results in "group think" and stasis.

The growth of reliance on standardized, measurable outcomes has increased reliance on test scores, thereby altering and limiting the definition of an educated person to reading, writing, and mathematics test performance. The fine arts, citizenship, critical and divergent thinking, and culture have taken a backseat as a means to comply.

What has been the impact of this increased role of the federal government through mandates, regulations, and incentives? Today, NCLB has been widely repudiated, but the role of the federal government continues to increase through carrot-and-stick approaches to push states to develop reform plans that mirror the federal department's initiatives. But the track record of federal reforms is not good, and American schools are not as bad as reformers portend. Michael Lind writes:

> To begin with, the U.S. public school system is hardly the abysmal failure portrayed in the conventional wisdom. The international comparative data is skewed by vocational tracking in Europe (all American high school students are sometimes compared to select gymnasium and lycée students in Germany and France) or geography (the entire U.S. is compared to the Shanghai metro area, rather than to all of China—the French educational system would look pretty bad, if it were compared in its entirety to Westchester County, New York).[14]

Diane Ravitch, in her book *The Death and Life of the Great American School System*,[15] recants her support for federal accountability, testing, and choice after having been a major architect of these supposed innovations to "fix" public education. In addition to these often-misguided policies it seems highly disingenuous for the Obama administration to talk about improvements and high standards while the financial house of cards of school financing is crashing. With the fiscal crisis at the national level, financial support from the federal government for supporting their reforms is not a good bet. And even at federal-level funding around 8 to 9 percent of all educational expenses, the federal government is hardly providing the level of support needed to meet all of its requirements.

Can innovation and discovering better ways to educate kids be mandated through federal reform options, as these recent proposals require? Can you name a continually adaptive and uncomplicated federal program? Are metrics from test scores the best indicator of having schools that produce children with the creativity, wisdom, and character to face a future that demands those qualities? Will Education Secretary Arne Duncan's ideas produce children who are "well schooled" but "poorly educated"? We don't think the federal government has been successful, and we fear the result is a "poorly educated" public.

In light of the public's view, the federal education department's role should not be directing the states on how to improve schools. Maybe the federal education department is an expendable, redundant, and costly federal agency that should be downsized to what its role was in the 1960s or eliminated. A better federal role would be to provide funds to conduct research, share ideas, and link school districts trying creative and innovative approaches to teaching and learning, or provide no-interest loans to impoverished districts for capital improvement projects thereby freeing money for instructional programs.

We believe that deeper federal involvement only results in more mandates, expanded centralized bureaucracy, and complicated and expensive initiatives, complete with their own jargon and reports, requiring more staff at the local level. Paying for all of this takes away scarce funds that could otherwise be put into reducing the preparation gap. Look at how No Child Left Behind diverted local energy and resources, took time away from instruction and spent it on test prep, limited the scope of the curriculum, and cut some programs that emphasize complex thinking, creativity, and imagination in favor of rote responses. The so-called race to the "nebulous top" is not much better in our view.

At a time when education needs innovative and imaginative solutions to educating all children, moving the locus of control away from local communities to the "Feds" only results in unnecessary, rigid, burdensome directives and regulations as the bureaucracy justifies its existence. If the bottom line result was positive we would not feel so strongly about these issues, but the past thirty years or so has not worked out that well.

In addition to the rush to condemn public schools, there has been a focus on certain achievement data that has been loosely interpreted or in some cases "cherry picked" with false comparisons being made about impact. Certainly there are problems and issues concerning American education, particularly with children in poverty who are facing other social and economic issues. But these truths are often lost in the flood of reports, headlines, and misinterpretation of the tests themselves.

Today, under No Child Left Behind and the Race to the Top, federal involvement has taken the form of coercive mandates based on the philosophy that the system needs to be manipulated, controlled, and incentivized to achieve a limited and narrow set of goals. Basically this means that if state and local governments want federal funds, they must do what the federal Department of Education wants to do concerning school reform. Thus, the increased involvement of the federal government and mandates emanating from the state has placed a straitjacket on discretion at the local level and the ability of the states to act as greenhouses of innovation and productivity.

NOTES

1. Diane Ravitch, *Left Back* (New York: Simon & Schuster, 2000).
2. Ravitch, *Left Back*, 459.
3. David Berliner and Bruce Biddle, *The Manufactured Crisis: Myths, Fraud, and the Attack on America's Public Schools* (Reading, MA: Addison-Wesley, 1995).
4. National School Board Association, "Myths and Realities in Public Education," www.NSBA.org/advocacy/myths-and-realities-in-public-education.pdf
5. U.S. Department of Education, *10 Facts About K-12 Education Funding* (Washington, DC: Author, 2005), www2.ed.gov/about/overview/fed/10facts/
6. U.S. Department of Education, Mission statement, www2.ed.gov/about/what-we-do.html
7. National Commission on Excellence in Education, *A Nation At Risk* (Washington, DC: U.S. Government Printing Office, 1983), available at http://datacenter.spps.org/sites/2259653e-ffb3-45ba-8fd6-04a024ecf7a4/uploads/SOTW_A_Nation_at_Risk_1983.pdf
8. Carl Levin, "Issues: Education,"www.carllevin.com/issues/education/
9. Patrick Leahy, "Education," www.leahy.senate.gov/issues/education
10. Russ Feingold, www.Feingold.senate.gov/record/cfm?id=320027
11. States News Service, "As Wisconsin Students Return to School Feingold Rolls Our Education Initiatives," September 1, 2010, *HighBeam Research*, www.highbeam.com/doc/1G1-236173803.html
12. Leahy, "Education."
13. Barak Obama, "Remarks by the President on Education," White House Office of the Press Secretary, July 24, 2009, www.whitehouse.gov/the-press-office/remarks-president-department-education
14. Michael Lind, "Education Reform's Central Myths," *Salon*, August 1, 2012.
15. Diane Ravitch, *The Death and Life of the Great American School System* (New York: Basic Books, 2010).

Chapter Three

The Narrowing Corridor
Why Deregulate?

Contrary to popular opinion most public schools work. American education is not a blatant failure that needs coercive hyper-regulation and mandates. Achievement data is skewed, especially in urban settings, where poverty and other social issues are strong issues in student performance.

> "If you look at the facts, then, they don't suggest that the U.S. public K-12 system is a failure. Rather American public education is a world-class success except among poor natives and immigrants, whose educational challenges have more to do with poverty and rural cultural legacies than alleged failings of public K-12. . . . The overall PISA (Program for International Student Assessment) scores of American students are lowered by the poor results for blacks and Latinos, who make up 35 percent of America's K-12 student population. Asian-American students have an average score of 541, similar to those of Shanghai, Hong Kong, Japan and South Korea. The non-Hispanic white American student average of 525 is comparable to the averages of Canada (524), New Zealand (521), and Australia (515). In contrast, the average PISA reading score of Latino students is 446 and black students is 441."[1]

The problem associated with too much testing, well documented by Berliner and Nichols,[2] and which Secretary Duncan noted when he acknowledged the failure of No Child Left Behind, is that our nation's preoccupation and almost single-minded focus on testing creates "perverse outcomes," unfairly labeling schools as failures, which creates a negative spiral of lagging support, decreased resources, and diminished public confidence, just when the opposite is needed. Although it is politically popular to scapegoat schools, calling them failures and blaming teachers and teacher unions, the truth is that most schools work and even the Gallup Poll indicates that most people feel that their local schools "are good."

Thus, popular public opinion seems at odds with President Obama's education reform plans that are largely achievement test–driven. While Education Secretary Arne Duncan and various pundits claim American education is failing and in crisis, local citizens see things differently. Phi Delta Kappa has been polling about education for forty-four years.

According to the latest Phi Delta Kappa (PDK)/Gallup Poll concerning what Americans think about their public schools, 49 percent give their schools a grade of A or B, and 89 percent give them a C or better. Only 5 percent thought they deserved an F and 11 percent gave them a D.[3] These numbers haven't changed much since 2005. Congress and the president should have such popularity numbers!

However, when Americans grade the schools nationally, only 18 percent gave the public schools an A/B and 71 percent gave them a C or better. Six percent gave the public schools an F and 20 percent gave them a D. This is quite a discrepancy from their perception of their local public schools.

No one argues that there are some poor schools that do not meet the needs of children. Nor do people believe that all teachers are stellar and deserve to be in today's classrooms. But this annual Phi Delta Kappa poll demonstrates that citizens view their local public schools positively; a much different narrative than what comes out of Washington.

Why such a difference? From a national perspective presented in the media, these poll results are not surprising. When it comes to their children, parents, grandparents, and relatives would rather work with local schools and the officials they know than have control rest in mandated approaches coming from the secretary of education's office or even their state department of education. Local school boards are closer to them.

Parents know their teachers, principals, and school board members and have direct, unfettered contact and influence about their child's education at the local level. Would you want your child's educational program in the hands of Congress and the faceless bureaucrats in the Department of Education? Local government is distinctive when it comes to education and is reinforced by the Constitution where education was relegated to the states. Centralized control creates geographical and interpersonal distance.

Concerning charter schools the PDK poll found that public support declined from 70 percent in 2011 to 66 percent in 2012. There is a large partisan divide over this issue, with 80 percent of Republicans supporting charters, compared to 54 percent of Democrats. Respondents were also divided on school vouchers, with a minority of 44 percent supporting the concept while 55 percent oppose.

On teacher evaluations that include student standardized test performance, the public is also divided. A small majority, 52 percent, favors including standardized test data, while 47 percent oppose. Of those favoring including student test scores in teacher evaluations 14 percent indicate that it should involve less than one-third of the total evaluation, 48 percent indicate it should involve one-third to two-thirds of a teacher's evaluation.

Three of four Americans have confidence in teachers: a far cry from the pillorying of teachers that has taken place in the media and from some reformers. When asked what qualities significant teachers had in their lives, the most repeated qualities (in order of most frequent) were: caring, encouraging, attentive/believed in me, strict/tough/discipline, challenging/demanding, good/great teacher, and committed/dedicated, and me. These are not characteristics that can be measured on a student achievement test.

While some reformers criticize teacher performance as one of the major issues facing schools, the public has a different perspective. According to the PDK poll the biggest problem facing schools is financial support at 35 percent. Ten years ago, discipline concerns (fighting, gangs, drugs) were identified as education's biggest problem. Today, the second largest concern is lack of discipline (8 percent), followed by crowded schools (5 percent).

In addition, Americans have significant disagreement with the administration about the role of the federal government in education and President Obama's "Race to the Top" reform agenda. Overwhelmingly, citizens see education as the province of state and local government, not the federal government. Concerning accountability, 80 percent see it as a state and local responsibility. The same is true for paying for education 79 percent, deciding what should be taught 71 percent, and setting standards for what children should know 64 percent.

Citizens reject Duncan and Obama's "Race to the Top" reforms. As to so-called failing schools 83 percent reject replacing the principal and staff, or closing the school and transferring the students (89 percent) (as they attempted to do in Central Falls, RI, in the spring of 2010 creating unnecessary disruption to students, families, teachers, and administrators only to reverse their actions after court proceedings) or closing the school and reopening it as a charter (87 percent). However, 54 percent indicated that the school should open with the existing teachers and principals and get comprehensive support from outside to improve it. Forty-four percent of the public recognizes that increasing teacher quality is important in improving education.

In these times, Americans see funding as the number one challenge facing public schools. Maybe the proposals for the "Race to the Top" were really a "dash for the cash" rather than a dedication to the original principles prescribed in the competition. With states being fiscally strapped as a result of the Great Recession and the federal money so attractive, states had little choice on taking a gamble by accepting coercive reforms.

In urban education we need to ask the fundamental question about whether it is the schools that have failed or whether social policy has failed. In Connecticut, a state with the largest achievement gap in the nation, it is fair to ask why so many students come to school completely ill-prepared to attend to work, have virtually no preschool skills or experiences, and have parents who themselves are limited in their educational backgrounds, and what impact this all has on school success. We know, for example, that if a child is not reading at proficiency rate by the end of grade three that child is likely to drop out of school. But how is a child expected to read by third grade if they come to school lagging years behind with little support at home and in classes that are overcrowded? How are children supposed to learn when they come to school hungry or frightened because of violence in their neighborhoods? Why aren't the policy makers focusing on the preparation gap as much as they are on the achievement gap?

In a recent *New York Times* article titled "Investments in Education May Be Misdirected,"[4] Eduardo Porter reports on a speech by James Heckman, a Nobel laureate in economics, before the Nebraska Chamber of Commerce, where he demonstrated that the United States is second to last in early childhood spending among the nations studied. The article asks whether we are starting too late: "Studies show that disadvantaged children gain the most from preschool attention. But government spending on the very young is much lower in the United States than in most other industrial countries." Heckman went on to point out that opportunity matters, that the achievement gap is "enormous" in the United States between rich and poor students and for children whose mothers did not attend college vs. those that did, from among the sixty-five countries participating in PISA.

WHY DEREGULATE?

It is clear to us that big government is not up to the task of guiding education policy; just look at all the national calamities where governmental policy has failed to resolve the nation's problems. Take energy policy for example. Tom Friedman of the *New York Times* has consistently written both in op-eds and books about the need for the United States to leverage its entrepreneurial spirit to take the lead in green and renewable energy. But the nation still lacks a coherent successful energy policy. While we do have current education policy focused on reform, it is not working because it is misguided reform and it is not the answer to better schools.

We argue in this book for a set of guiding principles that will move us in a different direction. We believe that the government has gotten it mostly wrong since "*A Nation at Risk*" in 1983 and that government should move away from regulation to one of investing in innovation and entrepreneurial spirit and actions with fewer controls, not more. Given the wrong-minded intrusion of the federal government, particularly over the past decade, and noting that the Constitution cedes the role of education solely to the states, we argue that the role of the Department of Education should be severely limited.

Since most schools work even when focusing on narrow achievement test measures, we need to deregulate these schools further to allow for innovation and creativity to flourish. For those schools that do not work it is our contention that their challenges are largely due to preparation gap. How can one responsibly hold Central Falls (RI) high school teachers accountable for achievement when the poverty rate and mobility rate in their school is over 50 percent? How can we hold teachers in one elementary school responsible for "mastery" when students come to school hungry, ill-prepared and with a mobility rate of over 80 percent—meaning, that a first grade teacher who starts the year with twenty students will have sixteen new students by the end of the year?

In a recent Stanford and Economic Policy Institute study by Martin Carnoy and Richard Rothstein, they stated, "You can't compare nations' test scores without looking at the social class characteristics of students who take the test in different countries. Nations with more lower-social-class students will have lower overall scores, because these students don't perform as well academically, even in good schools. Policy makers should understand how our lower and higher social class students perform in comparison to similar students in other countries before recommending sweeping school reforms."[5]

In these cases public policy should focus on why the preparation gap exists for entering students and develop policies to address the problem. As Heckman pointed out, we should invest more heavily in the earlier years of a child's life[6]—and it is our experienced view that these investments should begin at the prenatal stage and continue immediately after birth up to the age of kindergarten. However, doing so may not be that easy because of the avalanche of mandates that schools must address and scarce funding for any new initiatives. We argue for a loosening of this complexity to allow schools to really innovate.

Thus, current debate about public education misses a critical issue. Are students who are attending the public schools becoming well educated or well schooled? There's a difference—one that is seminal in determining almost every other discussion about public education.

EDUCATION VERSUS SCHOOLING

The current emphasis on test scores to determine school success has narrowed the definition of education. The assumption is: if children do well on standardized tests, then they are well educated. But that assumption is wrong. Here's why.

Take a look at Wall Street, where individuals with degrees from top colleges and universities cooked the books, reported deceptive metrics and bilked investors and taxpayers. This behavior largely caused the Great Recession of 2008. Yet, all of these Wall Street bankers obviously passed standardized tests and demonstrated acumen in reading, math, business, and finance. The question is: were they well-educated?

Or take Washington. Many prior presidential administrations were packed with the "best and brightest" individuals with Ivy League law degrees and doctorates who have demonstrated their knowledge of facts, concepts, and theories. The Nixon, Reagan, Clinton, and both Bush administrations had smart people who, in retrospect, made bad decisions (or at least wrong as tested by history), and in some cases even unethical and illegal ones. Recently we've seen some very questionable policy requirements coming out of Washington such as holding schools and teachers accountable for achievement scores when the link between root cause and outcome cannot be determined statistically or psychometrically (see chapter 5 for a more thorough discussion of this issue). If we did this same sort of thing in medicine, it would be called malpractice. Members of Congress, the vast majority with college degrees, feast at the trough of lobbyist money and succumb to vested interests. The question is: are they well-educated or well-schooled?

In these examples, individuals work in complex and high-pressure situations that call for more than literacy and simple mastery of facts or concepts. All of us live in an increasingly complex world that requires more than "smarts" or "shrewdness." What is necessary is wisdom and ethics, terms seldom heard today in discussions about education.

Today's schools are becoming pressure-packed places focused on producing narrow results, specifically in reading and math, on standardized tests. The emphasis on test scores, rank in class, grade point averages, or other numeric indicators has caused teachers to limit their focus and prepare students for these tests. An inordinate amount of time is spent on teaching test format familiarity, test-taking skills, and drill. Other subjects—history, science, and the fine arts—are being squeezed out or curtailed as a result especially when resources are being cut. And then we must ask, what does it mean to be a good citizen? What principles will guide the decisions you make in your life? Where are those outcomes on the state mastery tests?

Appropriate achievement tests are helpful if they assist teachers in making sound prescriptive instructional decisions for individual students. One-time, high-stakes test events, however, can compromise time for creative and imaginative lessons that promote reasoning, problem solving, questioning, analyzing, synthesizing, and understanding.

Consequently, we are teaching students the "game of schooling" as if it were a short-term competitive exercise—do what you must to get the number you need. Hence, many high school students are concerned with passing, not learning; short-term grades, not in-depth understanding; and building résumés, not following their passion. Principles and ethics are not on the radar screen. Sounds too much like the ethics and past practices of Wall Street to us. And these issues are now contributing to a growing anti-test movement in the United States.[7]

We are teaching that competition is the only approach to reaching excellence, as if principles, commitment, and hard work do not matter. We deliver the message that human worth can be quantified by a set of numbers, discounting the intangibles of "heart," perseverance, and steady commitment.

The idea seems to be that what is not metrically measurable is not important—a cousin to the idea that if you cannot see it, don't believe it. This flies in the face of the very concept and principles under which this country was founded.

The great philosophical questions of life—truth, beauty, justice, liberty, equality, and goodness—cannot be assessed by a computer-scored test. There is no real metric for them. Searching for answers to these issues is at the very core of our society and the essence of becoming well educated.

To live a life of depth, understanding, and principle, students must contemplate and gain an understanding of these ideas. This requires a broad education in the academics, fine arts, philosophy, and culture. An education is more than simply getting a job or meeting a career goal. There is a difference, too, between education and training.

All of our children, rich and poor, should be educated so they can contribute to the common good, be responsible and active citizens, and adapt to changing times. Being able to think critically, to pose questions as well as seek answers, and to understand and develop an ethical and moral framework are a part of being well educated. Educated people have strong academic skills, but they also have the values and principles that form the foundation for their life's decisions. Wisdom is the goal.

Unfortunately, as a result of federal policy, many of our schools are becoming too narrowly focused and our competitive society has pushed some of our high school students to say "I have to cheat" to get ahead and some teachers and administrators to do the same to keep their jobs or gain bonuses. Cleverness, cunning, and cutting ethical corners are not standards of an educated person. The very recent allegations in Atlanta, Georgia, for example, where some thirty educators including the superintendent of schools have been indicted (as of this writing) for wide-scale cheating on achievement tests so as to gain large bonuses is an example of a perverse outcome of wrong-minded policies. To be fair, these are only allegations at this point in time, as these individuals have been indicted by a grand jury, but similar allegations are now surfacing around the country and are the types of behaviors that Nichols and Berliner warned about in their 2007 book *Collateral Damage—How High Stakes Testing Corrupts America's Schools*.[8]

Well-educated people revere knowledge and apply values and principles to guide them as they seek a meaningful life of purpose. They try to make "wise" decisions premised on strong ethical and moral ideals and broad academic understanding. Education is a lifelong process of continuous learning and examination—not a race. Being well-educated means having a sense of stewardship and a concern for the common good, not simply tending to self-interest and ego needs.

Parents frequently say they want their children to attend a "good" school. A good school is not one between excellent and poor. For children to grow, develop and prosper they need a place of "goodness"—a sanctuary for learning filled with respect for individuals, reverence for principles and ideas, encouragement of talent and dreams, and preparation for a life well lived.

If we ask ourselves the fundamental difference between being well schooled or well educated, maybe we can turn our schools into sanctuaries for our children to become not only highly literate but also wise so they can fulfill themselves and pursue their happiness with a sense of stewardship for the common good.

History shows that deeper federal involvement in local policy making only results in more mandates, an expanded centralized bureaucracy, and complicated and expensive initiatives, complete with their own jargon and reports, requiring more staff at the local level to address. Look at No Child Left Behind which diverted local energy and resources, took time away from instruction and spent it on test prep, limited the scope of the curriculum, and resulted in the cutting of some programs that emphasize complex thinking, creativity, and imagination in favor of rote responses.

As a society we need to realize that education is not a "race" and that centralized mandates will not produce imaginative and well-educated people. Education is more than passing tests, and responsibility for getting an education is shared between schools, parents, and students themselves.

A centralized bureaucracy in Washington is not the answer in nurturing well-educated, wise people of good character. Local control puts faces on accountability and emphasizes that parents, students, and educators are responsible for the community's children. Doesn't the phrase, "Hi, I'm from Washington and I am here to help" scare the hell out of you when the consequences affect your children?

THE NARROWING CORRIDOR

We believe that the most important issue today is the new realities that affect all school leaders in general. As a result of ever-increasing federal and state control, the "corridor" within which they have to manage and make decisions has narrowed significantly and the speed with which events unfold make the job tougher, requiring more knowledge, political skill, media savvy, and interpersonal skills. Educational leadership has changed dramatically over the past fifteen years or so, and not for the good. Educational leaders are more policy compliance officers today. There is little for them to "lead" since so much of their day, week, and year is spent in addressing the myriad of regulations and laws that now govern education. Table 3.1 gives some examples of how executive leadership in schools changed between 1997 and 2010.

Table 3.2 shows what has not changed.

This book is about the narrowing corridor public schools find themselves operating within, which is the result of the unanticipated consequences of the regulating, mandating, and legislating. We argue that for public schools to be truly successful, we need to deregulate them, roll back the mandates wherever possible and widen the decision-making corridor to allow the creative and innovative minds working in public education to do their best work. We believe that all children—from all socioeconomic classes—should be well-educated, not just well-schooled as currently defined by standardized achievement tests. In that regard, we must address the preparation gap and the nature of our goals for an educated citizenry.

Table 3.1.

Topic/Issue	1997	2010
Budgetary control	Finances tended to take care of themselves—few surprises during the year once budget was set	Must follow the money given likely deficits for special education, legal costs, unanticipated new legislative mandates; and unanticipated cuts in state aid at end of legislative season.
State role	Oversight—direction setting; helpful experts in the field	Regulatory; pass through regulation oversight from Feds pervasive. This mirrors the unprecedented influence of the Feds in local school governance.
Poverty	Present but not pervasive	Rising nationally and locally; 1 in 8 is now in poverty; students in distress. Goodwin[1] discusses what it will truly take to close the achievement gap—among the primary findings: provide whole-child supports to deal with family/student disadvantage and distress.
Preparation gap	Not in our lexicon	Ever-present pressure; too many kids ill-prepared for school. Districts are narrowing the achievement gap but cannot close it due to the preparation gap.
High-stakes testing	Not recommended; see 1999 National Academies Study[2]	Driving school personnel behavior; creating perverse outcomes.[3]
Role of Feds	Providing support through grants	Regulatory with disincentives.
Autonomy of local board, superintendent	Strong	Weak, given all the mandates and regulations.
Curriculum	Local/state balance	States now complying with federal requirement and new standards due to Race to the Top program application.
Charter schools	Just getting started	Mixed results; if charter schools are such a good idea, why not deregulate much of public education?[4]
Role of superintendent	Could more easily act as proactive leader to design and implement local solutions to instructional challenges	Needs to be careful not to be overreactive to all the pressures; needs to manage complexity to retain primary focus on the instructional core where possible; needs to ensure compliance with myriad of regulations.

[1] B. Goodwin, *Changing the Odds for Student Success: What Matters Most* (Aurora, CO: Midcontinent Research for Education and Learning, 2010), www.changetheodds.org/pdf/0125MM_CTOPub_sml.pdf

[2] Jay P. Heubert and Robert M. Hauser, *High Stakes: Testing for Tracking, Promotion, and Graduation* (Washington, DC: National Academies Press, 1999).

[3] Sharon Lynn Nichols and David C. Berliner, *Collateral Damage: How High-Stakes Testing Corrupts America's Schools* (Cambridge, MA: Harvard Education Press, 2007).

[4] See "Groups Eye Regulatory Relief Under NCLB," *Education Week*, November 15, 2010, www.edweek.org/ew/articles/2010/11/15/12esea_ep.h30.html

Table 3.2 What Has Not Changed in School Leadership

	1997	2010
Philosophical beliefs of educational leaders	Needs to have a well-defined philosophical position on various issues that can stand the test of a frustrated public and local, state and potentially national media.	No change in concept—we now describe this as a "Theory of Action," however, with a focus on the instructional core as the "main work" and ensure that all we do is coherent with that mission.
Leadership matters	Strong working leadership team of the superintendent and the board is critical; if the superintendent and board are constantly at odds, people in the organization will hunker down and take fewer risks.	No change.

NOTES

1. Michael Lind, "Education Reform's Central Myths," *Salon*, August 1, 2012.

2. Sharon Lynn Nichols and David C. Berliner, *Collateral Damage: How High-Stakes Testing Corrupts America's Schools* (Cambridge, MA: Harvard Education Press, 2007).

3. "The 44th Annual Phi Delta Kappa/Gallup Poll of the Public's Attitudes toward the Public Schools," *Phi Delta Kappan* 94, no. 1 (September 2012): 45–50.

4. Educardo Porter, "Investments in Education May Be Misdirected," *New York Times*, April 2, 2013.

5. M. Carnoy and R. Rothstein, *What Do International Tests Really Show about U.S. Student Performance?* (Washington, DC: Economic Policy Institute, 2013), www.epi.org/publication/us-student-performance-testing/

6. Porter, "Investments in Education May Be Misdirected."

7. John Tierney, "The Coming Revolution in Public Education" *Atlantic*. April, 25, 2013, www.theatlantic.com/national/archive/2013/04/the-coming-revolution-in-public-education/275163/

8. Nichols and Berliner, *Collateral Damage.*

Chapter Four

The Growing Impact of Regulation on Public Schools

Earlier we discussed the burgeoning role of the federal government in public schools. The purpose of this chapter is to demonstrate that increasing federal and state regulations are stifling local educators' ability to implement the very creative and innovative solutions to school problems the regulations are supposedly designed to enable.

Overregulation is not solely the bane of education; many other fields suffer the same lament. Phil Streifer was sharing his concern over the cost of a nursing home stay for his father during the later stages of his life with a colleague who operates nursing homes in the Northeast. His colleague estimated that over 30 percent of these costs are due to regulation. As the colleague tells it, someone makes a mistake at a nursing home in Ohio and the federal government writes a regulation affecting all nursing homes in the nation, thereby driving up costs for all.

Perhaps not well known to the everyday citizen is the similar burden placed on public schools with all of the local, state, and federal regulations piled on each and every year. Superintendents are interested to see what happens when local citizens, who are often elected to school boards on a single issue such as "public education costs too much," discover how little control they actually have over these costs.

Superintendents too have very little control over many of the functions that govern their schools. Budgets are almost completely established by regulation. For example, special education takes up between 25 and 30 percent of most school budgets yet these dollars only serve between 10 and 15 percent of the student body. Labor laws govern a myriad of issues such as how school districts negotiate with employee groups and hire, fire, lay off, and discipline employees, and local employment contracts (in states with right-to-bargain laws) often govern how they assign staff. A dissatisfied external applicant for a job can tie up a central office human relations department in a host of red tape and legal proceedings arguing age discrimination before the Equal Employment Opportunities Commission. A student unhappy with a disciplinary decision can take a case through the courts (in many states) arguing an infringement of their civil rights. With a move to federal standards in curriculum, local decision making as to what textbooks or curriculum should be used becomes limited, given that most textbook companies will comply with these standards to stay in business. And since most school budgets are comprised of teachers teaching around twenty-five students each, there is little left to be creative with.

Federal and state legislatures often pass legislation on the basis of one crisis or event. These statutes, in turn, affect every school district in the state, requiring, at the very least, additional paperwork but frequently additional programs and staffing. Thus, these statutes have financial implications, most of which must be assumed by the local property taxpayers. And, once passed, few pieces of legislation are ever rescinded.

One might simply argue that just as state and national governments enacted these laws creating all these regulations, they could easily deregulate. That is not so simple, however, and our experience tells us that deregulatory efforts typically run into a host of special interest groups that stall or kill forward movement. In Connecticut, for example, there were several attempts, including joint lobbying efforts by the state superintendent's association, the Connecticut Conference on Municipalities,[1] and others that did result in a commission being established to find ways to deregulate both local schools and governments. However, nothing came of this effort for the reasons stated here.

This is a national problem. Just how serious and intrusive is overregulation? In March 2011 the American Association of School Administrators (AASA) reported on Robert Grimesey's testimony before Congress on regulatory pressure. Grimesey, superintendent of Orange County Schools in Virginia, testified before the House Education and the Workforce Subcommittee on Early Childhood, Elementary and Secondary Education. Grimesey was one of four witnesses at the hearing, entitled Education Regulations: Burying Schools in Paperwork.[2] AASA reported that all of the witnesses, including Grimesey, highlighted the burden and overreach that the paperwork of education compliance represents. While questioning after the written statements diverged from the narrow topic of the hearing to include ESEA reauthorization, funding, the proper role of government in education, and the compounding effect of state and federal paperwork, the message was clear: paperwork represents a sizable burden to local school districts and warrants closer examination as the committee moves forward with ESEA reauthorization. (Note: ESEA is the Elementary and Secondary Act of Congress, originally passed in 1965, as part of the War on Poverty, which funds support programs for reading and mathematics.)

In Connecticut, the Connecticut Conference of Municipalities (CCM) reported on all of the burdensome mandates on local municipalities and school districts, quoting from an analysis Phil Streifer did for his school district detailing the mounds of regulations and paperwork weighing schools down.[3] This analysis details over three single-spaced pages of mandated programs and reports each school district must make to the state or federal government and the manpower costs required.

Appendix B has the full list of "unfunded" or "underfunded" mandates that impact the Bristol (CT) Public Schools budget, which was published in the CCM report. The cost of these mandates for Bristol alone was estimated at approximately $15,000,000 on a total budget of just over $100,000,000. Bristol's state and local revenues were either frozen or cut for the prior four years yet these mandates kept increasing. Table 4.1 below summarizes the impact of mandates.

Some of the individual mandates by themselves are not overwhelming in terms of their cost but in total have a tremendous fiscal impact. In this single district from only one year, $14.7 million amounts to roughly $1,674 per student (Bristol enrolled 8,800 students), which is almost 15 percent of the entire school budget. Smaller districts suffer the same impact and frequently must increase paperwork demands on their limited staffs or outsource some of their work, which increases the cost even further. As Streifer said publicly and in testimony many times, that $1,674 per child per year would go a long way toward closing the preparation gap. In smaller districts administrators spend a good deal of their time complying with these regulations taking important time away from instructional leadership.

Imagine if this manpower effort and their related costs were released to develop and implement creative and innovative solutions to school problems? Or, consider the value if these resources were applied directly to lessen the impact of the preparation gap? Instead, central offices, principals, and teachers are burdened with regulatory duties that distract from their core mission.

Table 4.1. Mandate Summary: Estimated Funds and Extended Costs for Bristol, CT, 2011

Mandate	Estimated Total Cost Including Local Labor Costs
Partially Funded	$7,549,694
Unfunded	$7,173,650
Total Cost	$14,733,344

And all this effort costs precious resources that take away from that core mission and adds paperwork, time, and ancillary staff to complete reports.

We recognize the right of legislative bodies to enact laws, but there are often serious unanticipated consequences of those laws. In the Bristol case, costly regulation takes away resources needed for "regular public education" programming, which is why class sizes were going up, schools were being closed to consolidate for savings, and music and arts programs were being cut back.

If regulations are truly necessary, then that regulating branch of government should pay for them. But that rarely happens in practice. Special education is a good case in point. No one we know of is against providing for students with special needs, but as former superintendents, we grow ever more concerned as these costs escalate and local revenues become squeezed, especially by the Great Recession. If special education programs account for 12–15 percent of the student body yet their costs represent 25–30 percent of the budget, then programs for the remaining 85–88 percent of the student body have to be cut or reduced. Eventually, this may pit regular-education parents against special-education parents as fiscal resources become even scarcer. Superintendents, as "officers of the state" simply cannot ignore the law, so they reduce where they can, where there is no prohibition or regulation from doing so.

Not all regulation is bad, and one can argue the merits of regulatory control sector by sector. In financial services, the "Great Recession of 2008" was created, many argue, by deregulation of the banking sector. The book *Too Big to Fail: The Inside Story of How Wall Street and Washington Fought to Save the Financial System—and Themselves* clearly details that national debacle.[4] In health care, as noted earlier, regulatory control is driving up costs beyond the country's ability to afford the very services these controls are meant to protect. In energy, regulatory control could be seen as beneficial especially when disasters such as the BP Gulf oil spill of 2010 occurs. But in education, where just about everyone is arguing that schools need to be creative and innovative, we have ample evidence that the growth of burdensome and costly laws and regulations is choking any chance of implementing imaginative solutions. We need the pendulum to swing back toward deregulation of education.

Just as we saw in Connecticut, where an effort to deregulate stalled, so too have efforts nationally. No Child Left Behind, which has been called a failure as we noted earlier, remains unchanged due to disagreement in Congress on how to proceed. The resulting costs for testing created by NCLB, which is assumed by local districts and states, is not often discussed but is significant as test publishers reap profits and schools must redirect funds and reduce other programs to pay for this short-sighted program. One report by the Brookings Institution calculates that states spend collectively $1.7 billion a year on student achievement testing.[5] While that may not seem like a lot on a national level, taken at the local level it adds up. In Bristol, Connecticut, which enrolled about eighty-eight hundred students in 2011, that would amount to about $300,000 ($34/student). Streifer noted that he could have done an awful lot with that $300,000 rather than have students take an end-of-year state test that told them little that they didn't already know.

Throughout all of this there is an endless debate going on as some advocate for delegating more authority to the states and also providing local school districts more autonomy and flexibility in the use of federal education dollars. Others argue that doing so will let schools "off the hook" and will weaken accountability. Here is one account of how difficult it is to move forward. And while these debates rage on, local schools are left dealing with burdensome and costly regulations that limit creativity, stifle innovation, and take already limited resources away from their core mission. The issue of providing more flexibility is not an easy one:

> Republicans and Democrats on the House Education and the Workforce Committee tried hard, but failed, to reach agreement on a bill to give local schools more options in using federal funds. Thus, it appears that the funding flexibility bill unveiled last week by Committee Chairman John Kline, R-Minn., is headed for another party-line vote. The bill extends to all school districts the flexibility currently allowed for rural districts and expands schools' uses for certain formula funds under the Elementary and Secondary Education Act. For example, school districts could use funds from the Teacher Quality State Grant program to purchase new computers or create a new literacy program for English Language Learners.
>
> Democrats think this is a terrible idea. Committee ranking member George Miller, D-Calif., called it a "shortsighted proposal [that] would allow chief state school officers and school district superintendents to siphon away money intended for poor and minority students." In a new report, committee Democrats outlined ways that schools can have flexibility in using federal dollars while maintaining the core elements of the federal role in education.
>
> Whose proposal is right? What is lost or gained if schools are given a great deal of funding flexibility but still must meet certain standards, as Republicans are proposing? Can schools operate efficiently within the constructs of the current law, as Democrats are suggesting, by utilizing the little noticed options already available? Is it possible to add more flexibility to schools' funding options and maintain the core tenets of No Child Left Behind? Or does it make more sense to worry less about the federal standards and hand the lion's share of the responsibility to states?[6]

Dan Domenech, executive director of the American Association of School Administrators, responded with a post, "Let Local Educators Make Decisions":[7]

> The American Association of School Administrators strongly endorses and supports Chairman Kline's funding flexibility bill. The school superintendents that we represent are frustrated by the growing federal intrusion in local education and by the carrot and stick approach that has characterized federal funding. Local school boards, superintendents, principals and teachers are in the best position to determine what is best for the students that they serve. The federal government wants to parlay the eight percent of funding they currently contribute to local education into total control of what happens at the school level. This lack of trust in the educational community is appalling and an insult to the hardworking men and women that have dedicated their lives to educating our youth. We do not shy away from accountability and we are not asking to be relieved from ensuring that all of our children, including the poor, the second language learners, our special needs children, receive the quality education that they are entitled to. The achievement gap between our haves and have-nots must be erased. But the system of threats and punishments that we have labored under with No Child Left Behind has not succeeded in closing the achievement gap. The threats of punishment have resulted in a test-based culture that at best has resulted in the deterioration of the comprehensive curriculum and at worst has led to unfortunate cheating scandals that can neither be condoned nor ignored. Place the decision in how best to use federal funds in the hands of the local educators and hold them accountable for meeting all the requirements that will ensure that all of our children are protected.

Whether more regulatory control is a good thing or not is primarily a function of one's policy perspectives, thus, one man's policy solution is another's overregulation. This entire issue can be distilled to one's orientation to policy questions such as:

- Should local schools be free to teach and operate as they see fit in meeting local community goals or are schools an instrument of national policy and thus should be controlled by the Feds?
- What is the real cause of poor educational performance? Ineffective teachers and principals or a growing preparation gap that many children have when they enter school? If it's bad teachers and principals, why do suburban schools do well while urbans do not? (We will demonstrate this point in the next chapter.)
- Are states going to be the policy makers as defined in the United States Constitution? If education is a state's right issue—why are the Feds so involved?

- Most funding for public schools is raised locally, thereby exacerbating income and wealth disparities. Why do we allow disparities in educational financing of public education from community to community, county to county? Why are so many state finance systems being challenged in court?
- If the Fed and the states enact mandates, shouldn't they pay for them in full?
- Since most funding for local schools is raised locally, why should the state and the federal governments exercise so much control?
- Can we protect students' civil rights while maintaining local community control over schools?
- Who really controls public schools? Local Boards of Education? The State? The Feds? What is the rightful role of a local board of education?

Regarding control over educational policy, the United States Constitution is clear, as noted earlier: education is not in the U.S. Constitution—it is a state's right. The answers to the other questions are difficult to come by but will drive the future of public education in this country. A relatively recent development to address flexibility is the advent of charter schools. Leaving the debate over the relative success of charters to others, it is clear that charters accomplish one goal that we write about in this book—enhanced flexibility and the ability of charter school designers to be more creative and innovative. Thus, charters would appear to address all of the fundamental issues we raise about the inflexibility inherent in public education policy today. That being the case, why not deregulate all schools?

HOW THE CORRIDOR HAS NARROWED

Streifer left the superintendency of a high-performing suburban district in 1997 to become a professor at the University of Connecticut. He returned to the superintendency ten years later in Bristol, Connecticut—an urban district. The main difference he experienced was not between suburban and urban issues, although these were clear. The main issue was how narrowed the decision-making corridor had become for all superintendents over those ten years. It is our view that local superintendents need more flexibility to lead and to innovate as charter schools have been provided.

Following are some examples that weigh down administrative staffs and limit their time and ability to innovate. These issues represent new restrictions that have developed between the 1997 period of "then" to the era of 2012 "now."

- Paperwork and reporting to state and Feds. Many central office administrators and school principals spend much of their time responding to state and national reports. (See the CCM "Mandate" list of paperwork requirements, appendix B.)
- Student discipline—controls on length of suspension and reasons for such. The rules governing student discipline have taken a great deal of flexibility out of the hands of local educators. True, many of these new rules were enacted due to irrational acts on the part of one or several schools. To ensure that similar transgressions do not happen elsewhere, state legislatures have enacted stricter rules about what can and cannot be done to students misbehaving. In Connecticut the legislature passed a law limiting out-of-school suspension, mandating instead in-school suspension. Many educators and others testified for and against this bill, but in the end it was enacted only to be suspended for a couple years due to fiscal constraints. In Streifer's testimony he argued that the transgressions of a few should not result in limitations for the entire state. He also argued that there would be unanticipated consequences from this law. For instance, his district had no staff or rooms available for elementary in-school suspension, thus elementary school administrators rarely suspended students, but now, with a mandated "designated space" and staff in place, they might be more likely to exercise the option. While Streifer could not condone the actions of his colleagues who irresponsibly suspended students on a regular basis, he felt the vast majority of more responsible administrators in the state were being punished for the acts of a few. Why is it, he asked, that when a transgression occurs, we find the need to regulate a solution for all rather than defer to the better judgment of the field as a whole? Of course at the heart of this issue is the question of whether we can protect students' rights without overcontrolling schools.
- Labor laws governing hiring, promotion, discipline, and termination. The labor laws in this country have become much more restrictive in terms of all aspects of the human relations functions of hiring, promotion, discipline, and termination. While it is certainly possible to terminate a "tenured" staff member, it is not easy and requires at least two to three years of serious documentation. It also requires that the individual under review be seriously deficient, not just mediocre. When a person is up for hire or promotion, we must document clearly and convincingly that no age or other discrimination took place if the individual is not recommended. Again, these laws and regulations were promulgated over transgressions in the field, but they have become overburdensome and should be relaxed.

- State departments of education have become highly regulatory, governing everything from improvement plans, turn-around plans, school improvement plans, teacher evaluation plans and programs, professional development plans and programs, response to intervention, student disciplinary plans, curriculum, and a host of other school functions. Back in the 1970s, 1980s, and even the 1990s, state departments of education could be called upon for help and technical assistance on a range of curricular and instructional issues because they had in their midst highly knowledgeable educators who were experts in their fields. That is no longer the case, as many of these folks have left the state level for local districts because of the regulatory nature of state department work or state workers are designated oversight and regulatory functions. Further, overall state department staffs are a lot thinner these days due to budget reductions requiring those remaining to do regulatory oversight.
- No Child Left Behind demanded a focus on those subjects that are tested, thereby narrowing the taught curriculum, especially in urban settings. In their recent book, *Collateral Damage: How High-Stakes Testing Corrupts America's Schools*, Sharon Lynn Nichols and David Berliner detail how teachers and administrators have either resorted to cheating at worst or have severely narrowed the curriculum (to save their jobs in what they see is a grossly unfair set of testing circumstances where students come to them with such deficits that they are unable to perform at the high levels expected due to their preparation gaps).[8] The curriculum has been narrowed so as to effectively eliminate any major focus on social studies, science, the arts, and other fields because these subjects are not tested. This narrowing of the curriculum will have a dramatic and long-term negative impact on the quality of the students graduating our schools.
- New national curriculum standards are now in place (called the Common Core) along with new testing programs that will soon focus on these new standards. This problem of what the standards should be, whether they should be devised nationally, by state, or locally, is a major issue in the country right now. Some thirty-five states have signed off on the new national standards. Yet these standards are not in all subject areas, and thus we will see more narrowing of the taught curriculum in the future, edging out the arts and other important subjects even further. With the coming of a new national examination/test focused on these national standards, we may see more of the unanticipated consequences of high-stakes testing that Nichols and Berliner documented as a result of NCLB. Thus, for local superintendents of school boards, the real decisions as to what is taught are no longer in their hands.

SUMMARY

Our experience tells us that over the past two decades or more the mounds of regulation have increased dramatically, thereby limiting what public schools can do. If we truly want public school teachers and principals to innovate on a scale large enough to make a national difference, policy makers need to reexamine their beliefs about regulation and control. Given where we have come to today in the daily lives of schools, teachers, students, and principals, the answer, we believe, is counterintuitive. If we want more creativity, we need to widen the corridor for teachers and principals to experiment without the fear of failure. We need a new definition of accountability and we need to provide adequate support and incentives, not sticks. Most importantly we need to provide the time and resources to be creative. That will only come when we get serious about deregulating American public schools.

NOTES

1. Connecticut Conference on Municipalities (CCM), *The State-Local Partnership for Public Education: An Unbalanced Relationship*, Public Policy Report (New Haven, CT: Author, 2011).

2. U.S. House of Representatives, *Education Regulations Burying Schools in Paperwork* (Washington, DC: U.S. Government Printing Office, 2011), www.gpo.gov/fdsys/pkg/CHRG-112hhrg65010/pdf/CHRG-112hhrg65010.pdf

3. Connecticut Conference on Municipalities (CCM), *The State-Local Partnership for Public Education*.

4. Andrew Ross Sorkin, *Too Big to Fail: The Inside Story of How Wall Street and Washington Fought to Save the Financial System—and Themselves* (New York: Penguin Books, 2010).

5. Mathew M. Chingos, *Strength in Numbers: State Spending on K-12 Assessment Systems*. (Washington, DC: Brookings Institution, 2012).

6. Fawn Johnson, How Flexible Can You Be? *National Journal*, July 11, 2011, http://education.nationaljournal.com/2011/07/how-flexible-can-you-be.php

7. Dan Domenech, *National Journal*, July 11, 2011, http://education.nationaljournal.com/2011/07/how-flexible-can-you-be.php

8. Sharon Lynn Nichols and David Berliner, *Collateral Damage: How High-Stakes Testing Corrupts America's Schools* (Cambridge, MA: Harvard Education Press, 2007).

Chapter Five

The Truth about Achievement and the Preparation Gap

Ever since the 1983 report *A Nation at Risk*, Americans have been led to believe that their schools are failing. The truth is that only some schools are failing and they are primarily those with large populations of poor children and students that entered with very large preparation gaps. If we want to solve the achievement gap problem we need to stop labeling all schools failures and put resources where they are needed to close the preparation gap.

Achievement tests are being used for many purposes beyond which they were designed, including evaluating schools and, lately, teachers. The truth is that any use of achievement tests beyond that for which they were designed renders those inferences faulty at best, and dangerously misleading at worst. Unfortunately educators themselves have been slow to take up this position, which has led to further misconceptions about the success of their schools.

In 1995 David Berliner and Bruce Biddle published a book titled *The Manufactured Crisis: Myths, Fraud, and the Attack on America's Public Schools* that essentially debunked every premise upon which the *Nation at Risk* report was based.[1] Berliner who was at the time, and still is, one of the most respected researchers in education, then embarked on a nationwide speaking tour spreading this message, but still very few educators had the courage to stand up to the false arguments being made about the public schools. So those misconceptions stood and became the commonly held view of many Americans.

We were both superintendents then and remember the issues brewing. Senator Chris Dodd of Connecticut spoke to local superintendents in the late 1990s cautioning that if we did not take control of the agenda, an external agenda would be cast upon us. We didn't, and then we wound up with No Child Left Behind, the largest single federal move to control state and local education in the history of the republic. Although maybe not its expressed purpose, the result was the further perpetuation of this misconception that schools are failing.

Of particular concern is the fact that the underlying psychometrics, or test construction issues, are complex, and very few Americans or even educators really understand assessment enough to refute the false arguments being made about schools. Too many educators as well as the general public are assessment illiterate. So false charges go unchecked and bad policy is enacted based on weak science.

In 2001 James Popham took up this issue with his book *The Truth about Testing: An Educator's Call to Action*.[2] An eminent author and psychologist, Popham identified several reasons why achievement tests should not be used to evaluate school districts, schools, or teachers. He has written several more volumes since on this topic including an outstanding 2010 work entitled *Everything School Leaders Need to Know about Assessment*, but his 2001 book stands out in our minds as a succinct explanation of the challenges we face in understanding how tests are often misused.

Most important of these reasons is the fact that achievement tests are designed to spread out test takers and this effort to create discriminating test items may eliminate test items that teachers have emphasized and students have mastered. Secondly, there is bias in these tests that works against poorer, disadvantaged students and those who do not have the native cognitive ability to easily answer some questions.

In his research for his 2001 book on several standardized achievement tests, Popham found that 65 percent of test items in language arts were linked to socioeconomic status while 45 percent were so linked in science and the social studies. In other words, poorer students would likely do less well on these items due to their lack of experiences (or in our view, their preparation gap).

Popham further found that many test items were linked to inherited academic aptitudes such as whether a student works easily with words or numbers or special relations. The percentages were staggering: 40 percent in reading, 35 percent in language arts, 20 percent in mathematics, 55 percent in science and 50 percent in social studies.

The technical term for this problem is "confounded causality" where the reason for a student doing well or not on a test may be related to factors other than what they were taught in school. That's not to say that they cannot do well, but if the test was primarily designed to spread out test takers and secondly if there are items that some students will naturally struggle with, it is hard to conclude that what a school does or a teacher does is primarily responsible for a student's score.

Popham notes something that most educators already know—that a student's home experience and wealth matter.[3] For example, a student who has few magazines and books at home will be at a disadvantage compared with those who do. A student who has not traveled with her family widely will be disadvantaged when test items refer to different cultures and parts of the country.

The Condition of Education,[4] a report of the National Center for Education Statistics, acknowledges these differences between groups by identifying percentages of students by subgroup and reporting their scores, including poverty and whether parents have resources such as books and magazines in the home and other factors. Unfortunately these subgroup results don't make the headlines, but our own review clearly shows that wealthier students and students whose homes include books and magazines really do much better than those who are poor or do not have ready access to such resources.

In both high-performing wealthy and poorer urban districts we can state unequivocally that these differences are real and that they matter when considering why some schools do well and others do not. And thus they will matter when evaluating teachers.

At the very heart of this issue is what we refer to as the "preparation gap." And while we're not saying that the achievement gap for poorer and less advantaged children cannot be closed, we do know that it will take longer and more resources to do so. Given the limited length of a typical school day and the pressures on teachers with larger class sizes, the preparation gap cannot be closed fast enough to close the achievement gap. That's because each year that a poor or disadvantaged student is in school, even if that student achieves an expected level of learning for that year, it is not enough to make up for the deficit. In our experience, a student would have to gain more than two years of learning each year of school over several years to close the achievement gap, given the preparation gap with which they started. And the further along they are in school (meaning the higher the grade level), the wider the gap is, requiring an even greater effort to make up the difference.

Now that No Child Left Behind has failed to "fix" American schools, a problem whose root cause is poverty and culture as measured by likely biased tests, we are about to exacerbate the problem by scapegoating teachers, as so many states are changing their teacher evaluation laws to require use of student test results as part of the evaluation system. That's wrong, it's unfair, it's unethical, and it's based on bad science.

In summary, Popham notes that the problem with achievement tests is not whether they are valid; rather, it is whether the inferences we make from them are valid given their limitations. *And therein lies the key challenge with using achievement tests to measure how well a school is performing or whether a teacher is effective.*

WHAT DO ACHIEVEMENT TESTS ACTUALLY TELL US?

This is a complicated question and one that is overly simplified by general media coverage. A typical state mastery test for a single grade level has many subtests covering many learning objectives. But all that is reported and used for No Child Left Behind "Adequate Yearly Progress" monitoring is the percent of students achieving a proficiency level as measured on a scaled score that is derived from a raw score in the major subject headings of reading, mathematics, language arts, and in some states science and social studies (although NCLB only requires reading, writing, and mathematics). Worse yet, in many cases with the advent of No Child Left Behind, the only thing reported was whether the school "passed or failed," that is, whether the required percent of students achieved proficiency in all subgroups, leaving a lot of detail hidden and not discussed.

No Child Left Behind essentially worked this way: Among all the grade levels and subject matter areas on a test, in order to "pass," a school had to reach a certain percentage of students attaining proficiency in each subject area, grade level, and subgroup. This included many subgroups, which each had to "pass," such as children in poverty and special education students. If only *one* subgroup in only *one* grade level on only *one* subject-area test failed to reach the required percentage of students who were proficient for that year, then the *entire* school was labeled a failure! This is primarily why President Obama and Secretary Duncan said No Child Left Behind needed revisions, because it was unfairly labeling good schools as failures.

Another problem with NCLB is that it measures different groups of students in a school, each year, as the comparison base. For example, if a school had three hundred third graders last year and two hundred fifty different third graders this year, NCLB measures what percentage of the new third graders reached proficiency as compared to last year's group. Test design limitations complicate comparing how last year's three hundred third graders did against how this *same group* of three hundred students did the following year as fourth graders. While it is possible to compute this "cohort" difference with some tests, it is not universally possible, so NCLB was written to require a "same"-grade-level comparison even though *different* students were being compared with one another.

In one school where Streifer was superintendent the teachers, principal, and parents had worked especially hard to get all their kids to the required level of proficiency on NCLB. They poured their hearts and souls into it with special afternoon, evening, and Saturday reading support programs and a lot of work disaggregating test results to focus on specific student learning needs. However, when the NCLB test results came out the school failed because of one subgroup—their special education students—that did not reach the required level of proficiency on one subject matter test. But the local newspaper headlines told a different story: the headlines read that this school and two others "FAILED" on No Child Left Behind. The staff and parents were devastated. The real failure was the report's integrity with the truth and underlying science.

In Connecticut it was very difficult to chart student cohort (or group) growth over time due to inherent limitations in test design, but the Bristol central office had been working on an algorithm to do so. When these headlines came out, student growth data were analyzed using this algorithm for all the grade-to-grade-level matched cohort/group comparisons that were possible with the test data from this school. In every single grade-level cohort comparison, students—in fact all students—gained at least a year's worth of learning over a year of instruction. When we presented these new results to the staff and parents they were extremely relieved because it demonstrated that their work had not gone for naught—they did have an impact.

No Child Left Behind uses achievement test scores to evaluate schools, which is just bad science, so even the reanalysis performed for this one Bristol school was groundless. The truth is that using student achievement tests for anything other than measuring what a student knows about a particular learning objective is wrong. But if the state was going to publish the fact that three Bristol schools failed, Streifer was intent on countering that wrong information, even though the underlying science was flawed in both cases. At times even superintendents need to be politicians!

Schools are much more than achievement test results. The typical level of parent, teacher, and staff effort in schools across the country is admirable, but it is not captured by these test results. Teachers' impact on motivating and inspiring students cannot be measured on tests. The warmth of the school atmosphere is not captured. How welcoming staffs are to parents is not measured. The visual and performing arts are not captured. And so on.

The bottom line is that the foundational science undergirding achievement tests simply does not support making summary judgments about schools without considering other factors as in the case of No Child Left Behind. Nor does it support evaluating teachers, but that is not stopping states from doing so!

TEACHERS, EVALUATION, AND TESTS

To understand why it's such a bad idea to evaluate schools or teachers using student test scores, consider a related field—medicine. We are always amazed at TV commercials for medications and the accompanying list of side effects. These typically air during the evening news, so you won't have to wait long to hear one for yourself, just tune in tonight. Given the strong side effects most of these medications have, it's a wonder that a physician would prescribe them or that anyone would take them. But given a pressing illness, there are acceptable trade-offs between the benefits and side effects of these drugs. The patient, understanding these trade-offs, makes an informed decision, as did the physician in prescribing the drug or procedure.

Now here is the key question: would you take a drug if you knew that the undergirding science used to prescribe it for your illness was flawed, even if there were no side effects? Would the physician prescribe it? Of course not; you wouldn't take it and the physician wouldn't prescribe it if only to avoid a malpractice suit, let alone violating the oath taken as a physician to "do no harm." Similarly, would you take a drug that had *no* evidence at all of healing your ailment? We wouldn't, and we don't think you would either. But by using tests improperly, we are committing this kind of educational malpractice.

The science used to create achievement tests simply does not support their sole use to evaluate schools or teachers—period. There are no equivocations here—you just can't do it because the inferences we make about schools and teachers from these tests are not valid.

Unfortunately, however, our nation has a habit of enacting unworkable or fundamentally bad policies in the name of "fixing" the public schools. As discussed earlier, the 2001 No Child Left Behind Act was the latest big mistake, with President Obama and Secretary of Education Duncan recently declaring NCLB flawed because, despite its good points, it unfairly labeled too many good schools as failures.[5] Now we are about to do the same thing to hardworking teachers.

NCLB led to even more perverse outcomes, including cheating by some teachers and principals.[6] What will this latest focus on unfairly evaluating teachers with achievement tests potentially lead to?

As we were writing the final drafts of this book to send to our publisher news broke out of Atlanta, Georgia, where the superintendent (who became national superintendent of the year for achieving uncommon student achievement results) and about thirty other educators have been indicted by a grand jury for a broad-based scheme to cheat on student achievement tests to win major bonuses. The defendants are claiming their innocence at this point in time, but in reading the full report that led to the indictment, it is hard to see how these individuals could not have been involved in some sort of scheme to erase incorrect student responses on tests. The courts will eventually decide the Atlanta case, but other prominent cases are now emerging, such as in Washington, D.C., where PBS's *Frontline* did a full-length story on Michelle Rhee's leadership style as superintendent that some say led to similar cheating on student achievement tests by teachers and principals to keep their jobs.[7] This is just the sort of thing Nichols and Berliner, as well as Daniel Pink,[8] warned about in their books.

There is an even more insidious problem here beyond the obvious. Organizationally, people will focus on what impacts them the most, and if a district administration is worried about a few test score points, professionals in that organization will focus on that problem. Principals and teachers will then do what they must, which can range from a single-minded focus on teaching what they think will be on the test to perhaps the type of cheating chronicled by Nichols and Berliner and which has now led to a major indictment in Atlanta, Georgia.

Doing what they must can include an ethically questionable practice of "educational triage." In an article, Mathew Springer discusses educational triage:

> Increasingly frequent journalistic accounts report that schools are responding to No Child Left Behind (NCLB) by engaging in what has come to be known as "educational triage." Although these accounts rely almost entirely on anecdotal evidence, the prospect is of real concern. The NCLB accountability system divides schools into those in which a sufficient number of students score at the proficient level or above on state tests to meet Adequate Yearly Progress (AYP) benchmarks ("make AYP") and those that fail to make AYP. The system gives no credit to schools for moving students closer to proficiency or for advancing already-proficient students. If schools intent on meeting minimum competency benchmarks practice educational triage, they dedicate a disproportionate amount of their limited resources to "bubble kids," students who might otherwise perform just below the proficiency threshold. While these marginally performing students are likely to benefit from increased attention, reallocation of instructional attention leads to a tradeoff whereby the achievement gains of the marginally performing students come at the expense of both the lowest- and highest-performing students.[9]

The laws and policies we put in place to improve education often have unintended consequences. Most troubling is the fact that these laws and policies can become a serious distraction from the primary work, which should be improving the instructional core—what highly effective teachers do with students using rigorous content.

THE PROBLEM WITH AVERAGES

Let's say for a moment that we *could* devise a test free from the problems discussed in this chapter. That is, let's assume that we had a test where we could reliably evaluate schools or teachers with high validity (without getting technical, validity refers to accuracy and reliability refers to consistency of results). The next problem is which scores to look at to truly understand how well that school or teacher performed.

In almost all cases, including the Nation's Report Card, results are reported as the "average" performance by some group of students on a subject matter test. However, anyone even minimally trained will know that we should never base decisions on simply the average because it tells us little of central tendency (how the midpoint actually did) without other important measures that help to explain the score, such as standard deviation (variation), median (midpoint), and mode (the score that reflected the most number of students).

Take a simple example that everyone can relate to—your annual income. Let's say we have ten people in a group and nine of them earn $75,000 a year while the tenth person earns a lot more—$250,000 a year. The average for the group then is the sum of all their incomes divided by the total number in the group—10. So, 9 × $75,000 = $675,000 + $250,000 (the tenth person) = $925,000 / 10 to get the average = $92,500. The fact is that the average of $92,500 does not describe reality for any of these ten people. For the nine who make $75,000, their world would be very different if their annual earnings jumped by $17,500, and the individual earning $250,000 would be dramatically different earning $157,500 less!

Achievement test scores suffer the same problem that can lead to misinterpretation, where an "average" reported score likely does not represent how well students did in those schools without other information. Because such distortions exist, it is wrong to assume one knows the "truth" when looking at average student performance only.

Statisticians have a solution for this problem and it is called standard deviation. But standard deviation is rarely reported or even considered when reporting test results. What we see in the newspaper headlines is that School A did not improve from last year or that School B did better than School A. But in reality, when we consider standard deviation, that interpretation may be flat out wrong. It may also be correct. The problem is that we don't know with the limited information conveyed by the average alone.

Let's look at an example. The following graph shows the performance of two schools in the same school district on a state mastery test—reading.

The test in figure 5.1 is reported in what looks like an unusual range—from 100 points to 400 points as shown on the left or vertical axis of the graph. How, might you ask, can a test start at 100? Statisticians have a way of converting the original raw score (which is simply the number of test items correct) to something called a scaled score range that is more useful in a number of ways.

Suffice it to say that a test that might only have seventy-five test items can be converted to a scale such as this one. Confusing, yes, but that is part

The Truth about Achievement and the Preparation Gap 51

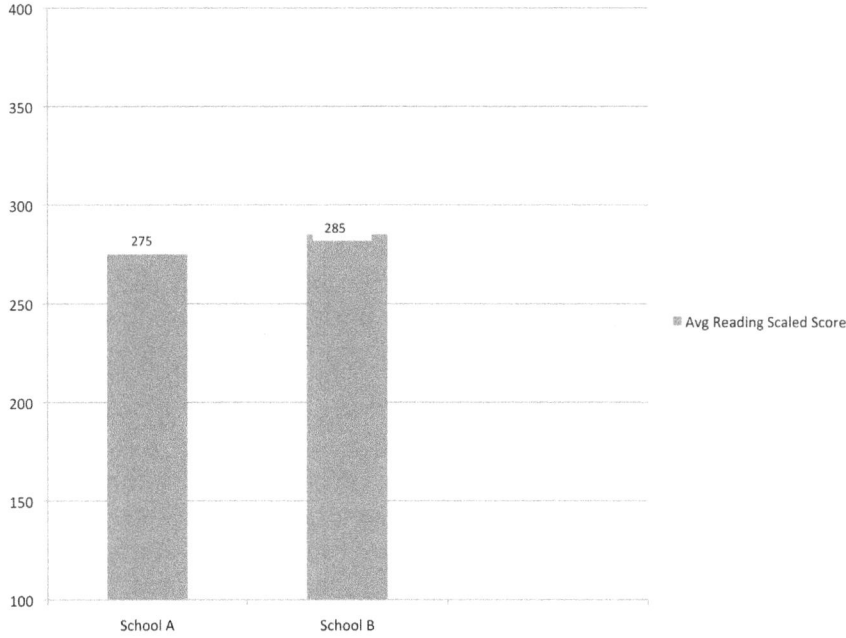

Figure 5.1. Average Reading Scaled Score

of the issue when trying to determine just how well students did on a test. Take for example something that many people are familiar with—the SAT or Scholastic Achievement Test. That test is reported on a scale that goes from 200 to 800—or a range of 600 points from what is essentially zero correct to a perfect score. But we all know that there weren't 600 items on the reading or math SAT test!

In our example above in figure 5.1 it looks as though School B outperformed School A by 10 points. And by just looking at the average, that is a correct interpretation. But there is more to the story that needs to be told.

Standard Deviation is the amount that scores vary around the average. If one standard deviation equals 40 points, for example, it indicates that about two-thirds of the group varied +40 points to –40 points around the average score. So, if the average was 275 and the standard deviation is 40, it means that two-thirds of the group in that school had scores between 235 and 315—or a total spread of 80 points. That's a lot, and it is a big difference from just looking at the average. Just like in the case of annual income, the average in this case does not represent reality for the students well below or well above the average score but within only one standard deviation. If we counted two or three standard deviations, then even more students would be outliers from the "average."

If the standard deviation for School A is 40 but the standard deviation for School B is only 20, what does that tell us about how these two schools performed—was there any meaningful difference between them? And by the way, this is a typical finding—the standard deviation will vary widely from school to school because it is a calculation on how all of the students in that school vary around that school's mean or average score. If a school has a higher number of special education or poor students who typically do less well, or a higher number of students from wealthier families who tend to do better, the standard deviation between the two can vary a lot.

Let's look at that same comparison but this time chart the standard deviation to see where two-thirds (one standard deviation) of the students in each school fall on the test score range.

The picture of achievement between these two schools is now more confused. The graph in figure 5.2 is attempting to convey how each school did overall, but looking at the spread of where two-thirds of the students performed (or one standard deviation denoted by the arrows) it appears to show

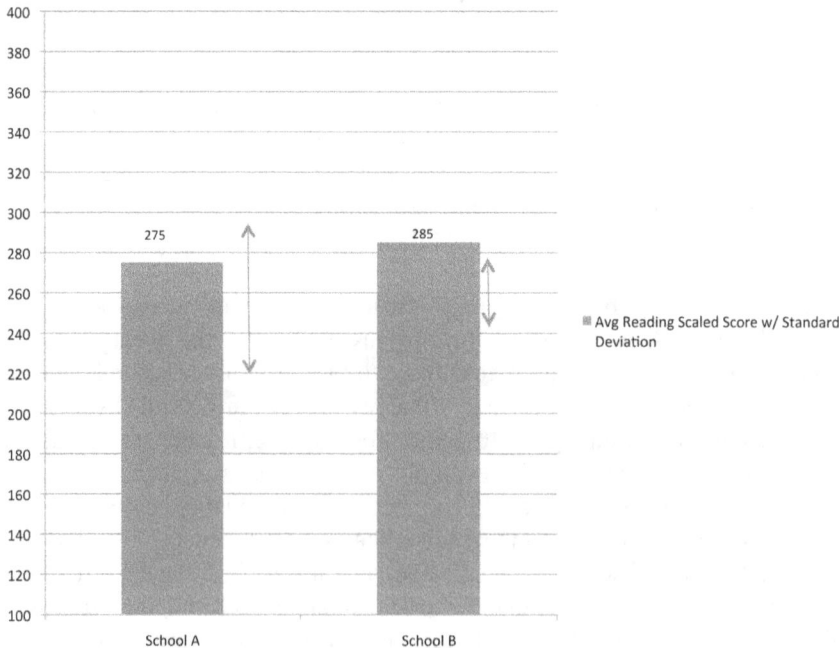

Figure 5.2. Average Reading Scaled Score with Standard Deviation

that there were actually more students in School A that outperformed School B within this two-thirds group.

Conversely, there were more students in School A that did more poorly also within this group. And if the students performing better in School A had been doing more poorly the year before, that would be quite an accomplishment! Another way of looking at this is that School A had a more diverse group of students, while School B had a more homogeneous group. Anyone who has taught in schools will know that it is much harder to teach a diverse or heterogeneous group of students than one more alike in total makeup.

But the fundamental point here is that we now have a much different picture of how each school did on this test than when just looking at one number alone, the average. At the very least it is impossible to say that School B outperformed School A. And if we called School A a failure, as No Child Left Behind often does, it would seriously misrepresent all the students who did well on the test.

Let's assume for a moment that the cutoff score for proficiency on this reading test is 275. Under NCLB, School B would likely be safe because most of their students fell well above the proficiency score. That is, a large percentage of their students were at or above the cutoff score. We can see why School A might be called a failure for having more students below that point. But they have many students above that point too. As the standards were raised by NCLB over the years (the proficiency score kept rising and a school needed more and more students reaching that level of proficiency), we can see why wealthier suburban schools tended to do well early on while those with poorer and disadvantaged students "failed" under NCLB. But these schools did not get credit for all the good they were doing on a year-to-year basis. And nowhere here have we talked about growth and gains of a specific group of students or a "matched cohort." It could be that even the very lowest performing students in School A gained a year's learning from the prior year but because they were below the cutoff, the school failed as a whole.

It would be nice if the underlying science of achievement test construction was so well developed that we could just trust these tests to work in all conditions. For example, we don't have to worry about our cars working when it's cold, when it's hot, or raining. And we don't have to understand how or why it works. Very few of us understand or even know "what's under the hood" other than to say there is an engine there and that we need to check the oil now and then and fill the windshield washer fluid.

We can't take such a lackadaisical attitude when it comes to student achievement tests if we want to be mostly right in their interpretation and use. Policy makers owe it to the profession (and even to their own reputations) to know how these tests work and to restrict policy initiatives to the limits of the tools such policies are based upon. Popham writes that "because an achievement test would seem to measure what students achieve—that is, what they learn in school—it's natural to perceive it as a suitable measure of what kids have been taught in school. . . . that perception is plumb wrong."[10]

EVALUATING TEACHERS AND VALIDITY AND RELIABILITY

The latest national trend is to evaluate teachers using student test results, and all the problems we've discussed so far apply here as well. The only inference we can draw from a student achievement test result is how well a student did on that particular test—not whether a teacher is doing a good job.

Two big ideas in psychometrics underlie this problem and Popham's caution. These have to do with how well a test actually measures what it was intended to measure and whether it does so consistently. The technical terms for these ideas are validity and reliability.

Let's say you want to test whether a student knows vocabulary and let's say that there are twenty items on that vocabulary test. If a student gets a zero, technically it only means that this student did not learn these twenty words, but certainly they know other vocabulary words. Conversely, if a student got 100 percent correct it only means that they know these twenty words and may not know other more important words. While this is a simple example, the concepts are the same as applied to all student achievement testing.

This leads to another key question—whether these twenty vocabulary test items are the most important and whether they should be used to ascertain that a student "knows vocabulary." In this example it would be correct to say that a student knew or did not know these twenty vocabulary words, but it would be incorrect to say that the student knew vocabulary or did not. The test only measures these twenty items and cannot be extended to a broader interpretation without further review.

Well, that is only partially true in this world of complex issues. If a panel of experts decided that these twenty vocabulary words were the sum total of what a student needed to know for promotion or graduation, then, yes, we could say that the student "knows" vocabulary as defined by these experts. And this is how it is actually done for some tests. There are complications, however, as Popham noted in his 2001 book and that we discussed earlier. If this is a particular type of test that is attempting to measure mastery, absent the goal of discriminating among students, then it is correct and proper to say they "know vocabulary" if they get these items right. But if it is a different kind of test that sets out to discriminate students along a continuum, then it would be an unfair and incorrect inference. Sounds complicated? Yes it is, and that's why assessment literacy is such an important issue in the interpretation and use of any of these tests.

The next question is whether this twenty-item vocabulary test yields the same results across all students. What if many of these items required a cultural orientation to city life, or rural life, or farm life? And if city life, a test item using a word such as "gridlock" in the context of getting to a job interview on time for someone who lives in rural America just might not resonate and have the same level of meaning as for a child who has been late to school several times due to traffic congestion. This problem is related to *reliability* or the degree to which the test yields consistent results. Test makers work to ensure that test items are culturally neutral, but that is really hard to accomplish for all potential situations. And this is only one problem related to reliability. In mathematics, for example, a common challenge in developing word problems is constructing a test item that tests math analytical skills, not the child's ability to read and comprehend.

In order to control for validity and reliability, test makers go through many development stages that are time-consuming and costly. This process also narrows the scope of the test item to a very specific point or learning objective. Because test items are so narrow in scope, many psychometricians argue that tests should only be used for what they were created for—to assess the specific area of learning or knowledge. This is why Popham argues that achievement tests do not fairly or comprehensively assess what students learn "in school." The simple fact is that schooling is much more complex than what can be measured on even a well-constructed test.

So it is therefore illogical and wrong to evaluate teachers using these tests. But many states are gearing up to do just that; and by the time this book is printed, using student achievement tests to evaluate teachers may be a fairly common practice.

How crazy can this get? Teachers are hired based on their academic training, among other factors, and the courses/programs they have taken in college. Upon successful completion (and in some cases testing such as on the Praxis Exam) they are awarded a certificate to teach by their state. After they are hired, and if they work in a state that demands some portion of the local district yearly teacher evaluation system be based on student achievement tests outcomes, we have a problem. Casting aside the issues discussed above about validity and reliability, there are many teacher certification areas for which there are no student achievement tests, such as teachers of music, art, and world languages; school psychologists, instructional support teachers (who provide contextually sound professional development to teachers in the classroom); and so on. What do we do with these teachers when we only test in mathematics, English language arts, and reading (and in some states social studies and science)?

The answer, it turns out, is even more illogical, worrisome and unethical—they base the student achievement portion of these teachers' evaluation on the schoolwide average! But what if that teacher is not average? Even if she is "average," as we have seen, we should never base important decisions on simply the average. So now we have two problems. First, it is just wrong to infer teacher competence from a student achievement test, and second, we are now extending that error to teachers for whom there are no subject matter tests, so we will just use the overall school average! This is just wrong. Teachers have rights as employees; they should be evaluated through valid, reliable, and ethical assessment systems.

As crazy as it seems, policy makers are throwing reason to the wind here and basing these other teachers' evaluation on the schoolwide average *because that's all that is available.* That's like saying we are going to give the patient a medicine we know is for some other ailment because we don't have a medication for this particular illness. In medicine, that's called malpractice.

What can we do about this and how can we mitigate the impact? Despite the illogic of evaluating teachers using these tests, the practice will be litigated and likely sustained because the "process" is what counts in these matters, not the ethical substance. State legislatures have the right to legislate, and if a law is followed, it will likely stand up in court regardless of whether it is "right" or not. Thus the imperative moves to making sure that teachers are not unfairly harmed, and doing so requires that all involved know and understand assessment literacy. By understanding the limits of assessment we can steer clear of blatant misuse by strengthening the impact of the other components of teacher evaluation. Only then will we succeed in righting another policy wrong. Having said this, as pragmatists, our druthers would be to have these new laws repealed regarding the use of achievement tests in teacher evaluation.

THE PROBLEM WITH PERCENTS

Another common way test results are reported is the percent of students attaining a score such as "proficiency." The No Child Left Behind Act primarily used this method of score reporting. The goal of NCLB was that by 2014 100 percent of students would be proficient. (Never mind that each state had its own test, some much more rigorous than others, and its own method of determining what "proficient" meant—that is a discussion for another book.)

Most state NCLB score schemas go something like this: the Below Basic category is worse than is Basic, and Basic is a lower achievement level than Proficient, and Proficient is less proficient than is Advanced. So "proficiency" is not a top-level score. That is important, since states developed their own tests (or they buy one) and set their own level of proficiency for each grade level and subject matter tested. If a state chose a higher standard, fewer of its schools would likely pass NCLB early on. A lower standard led to many more schools passing in those states. This was a real problem with NCLB and remains so as of this writing, as the standards across states in terms of content rigor and testing standards varied to such a great extent.

Regardless of the standards set by each state, another major problem with this score-reporting schema exists that led to misleading interpretations. Each score band, such as "basic" and "proficient" represents a wide range of scaled score points (remember the example earlier in this chapter where a small number of actual test items were transferred to a scale score range of 100 to 400). So, from one year to another year, a school could have worked really hard moving students from the low end of the "basic" range to the high end of "basic" but because the threshold to "proficiency" was not reached, all of this improvement is lost in the analysis. From NCLB's point of view, the school made no progress. And in a case such as this one the school would get no credit for that enhanced learning; in fact, it would be hidden to just about everyone including the staff and teachers unless someone took the effort to cull out this information.

That is what happened with the Bristol school described earlier where the staff and parents become so dejected. These wide score bands mask, or hide, student learning growth within each band. The answer to this problem is to measure student gains or growth of a matched cohort (or group) of students from one year to another in the next grade level up using the scaled score points; not to report the percent of students that fall within these wide score bands of "basic" and "proficient," etc. But almost all the tests used by states for NCLB were not constructed in a way to allow for cohort growth and gains analyses, thus, it is just not possible to do so.

JUNK SCIENCE

Diane Ravitch, a respected educational researcher and lately a well-known critic of most of the prevalent so-called reforms today, has called value-added teacher evaluation "junk science," thereby calling into question the use of test scores and value-added scoring for teacher evaluation *even when it is possible to do so*.[11] We have already discussed the fundamental problem of using test scores for teacher evaluation, or school evaluation—that the inferences we draw from these tests are only valid for the purposes for which the tests were created. And these tests are not designed for evaluating teachers or schools. So, that is problem one.

Next, regardless of the inference problem, states are piling on to use these tests in new ways, called value-added methods to evaluate teachers. Value-added methodologies use various data points such as student demographics, like poverty, to predict how a student *should* do on a test. If the student meets or exceeds the prediction, the teacher is given credit, it not, the teacher is held accountable.

The fundamental problem here is that building a value-added methodology on top of a flawed system does not resolve the initial flaw; it only exacerbates it, which is one reason why Ravitch termed value-added methods of teacher evaluation junk science.

To make matters even worse, for teachers for whom there is no test and who are scored based on the school average, the travesty is unconscionable. And finally, as we've seen, using the average for any decision making without more information is extremely limiting even when all the other foundational factors are correct, which in this case, they are not.

Unfortunately, policy makers don't seem to care about these facts; their minds are already made up. Most distressing to us is how many good educators have been duped into going along with these bad policies so as to engage with the political system. But bad science is bad science—period. We can only imagine that educators are going along to get along and are guided by their own assessment illiteracy. No well-educated academic in assessment could ever make a case for such practice among the scholarly community. Any such decision-making methodology proposed to a scholarly journal would be thrown out for its ignorance. Or, as Ravitch said it best, for being junk science.

Can you imagine applying such bad science in medicine! Not only would it be a violation of the Hippocratic oath, it would constitute malpractice, likely causing people to be seriously injured or even die. But in education we seem to want to go on experimenting with teachers' and students' lives. Doing so is wrong and it should stop.

THE PREPARATION GAP IS REAL

If we want to improve achievement, we need to focus on where it is weak, which is largely among poor and otherwise disadvantaged students. Most suburban public schools are doing very well. Students who come from wealthy families do well. Students attending private and independent schools are doing well. And despite the so-called failing American Public School System since the 1983 *Nation at Risk* report, we have built the most successful economy in the world. The problem is not with the basic system; the problem is rooted in poverty and parental neglect (either intentional or unavoidable).

The best way to demonstrate that poverty is at the root of the problem is with the Nation's Report Card, which uses the National Assessment of Educational Progress, a test used across all states, unlike with NCLB, where each state created its own test and set its own proficiency standards.

The Nation's Report Card (otherwise known as The Condition of Education) is published yearly by the United States Department of Education, and the 2012 edition paints a very different picture than the pundits and politicians would have us otherwise believe. Parsing through the hundreds of data tables one comes on a curious set of findings. First, not all schools are "failing," in fact, many are doing extremely well, and second, private schools (which have much more freedom to be creative and innovative and typically have wealthy students) do better than public schools overall. Third, poor children, especially those from families without formal education past high school perform much lower than those from wealthy families with a college education. And children whose homes contain magazines do better than those that do not.

Now, none of this should be a surprise, but it does matter with regard to how policy makers conceive of school improvement strategies and how these are applied throughout the nation. The popular press and many politicians would have us believe that drastic actions such as closing schools and firing principals and teachers are needed in order to solve this problem of underachieving schools. And recent legislation in a number of states has enacted such measures as part of the federal No Child Left Behind waiver process. But the Condition of Education paints a very different picture. The following information clearly shows that in a number of ways wealthier students do better than poorer ones; students with more opportunity do better than those with limited backgrounds; students with educated engaged parents do better than those coming from families with less education; most schools across the country are actually doing very well; and urban schools with higher concentrations of poorer disadvantaged students do less well than suburban schools with wealthier students. Here is a quick summary of what is contained among hundreds of pages, tables and charts:[12]

- Mathematics
    - Wealthier students in fourth and eighth grade from 1996 to 2011 did better than poorer students.
    - Wealthier students in twelfth grade from 2005 to 2011 (the years for which there are data) did better than poorer students.

60   *Chapter Five*

  - ○ Children of parents who graduated from college in eighth grade (1990 to 2011) and twelfth grade (2005 to 2011) did better than children of parents that did not graduate from college.
- Reading
  - ○ Wealthier students in fourth, eighth, and twelfth grade from 1998 to 2011 did better than poorer students.
  - ○ Children of parents who graduated from college in eighth and twelfth grade (1992 to 2011) did better than children of parents that did not graduate from college.
  - ○ Children whose homes had magazines in fourth, eighth, and twelfth grade from 1992 to 2011 did better than homes without magazines.
- Dropouts
  - ○ From 1975 to 2009 high-income students had a steady dropout rate of 2.3 percent.
  - ○ Low income students over the same time period had a dropout rate starting at 16 percent in 1975 lowering to 7.5 percent in 2009. The very schools charged with being "failures" have succeeded in lowering the dropout rate of poor students but the rate is still three times that of wealthier students.
- Proficiency
  - ○ Fourth-Grade Reading: The average scaled score for schools with 0–25 percent poverty was 238—proficient. The average scaled score for schools with 76–100 percent poverty was 203. Wealthier students did better.
  - ○ Eighth-Grade Reading: Proficiency required a scaled score of 267. The average scaled score for schools with 0–25 percent poverty was 279—proficient. The average scaled score for schools with 76–100 percent poverty was 247. Students who read for fun every day scored, on average, 284—proficient. Students who never or hardly read for fun scored, on average, 255. Students with magazines in the home scored, on average, 272—proficient. Students without magazines in the home scored, on average, 261. Students whose parents did not finish high school scored, on average, 248. Students whose parents graduated college scored, on average, 275. Overall, wealthier more advantaged students did better.
  - ○ Twelfth-Grade Reading: Proficiency required a scaled score of 291. The average scaled score for schools with 0–25 percent poverty was 299—proficient. The average scaled score for schools with 76–100 percent poverty was 266. Students who read for fun every day scored, on average, 305—proficient. Students who never or hardly read for fun scored, on average, 275. Students with magazines in the home scored, on aver-

age, 294—proficient. Students without magazines in the home scored, on average, 281. Students whose parents did not finish high school scored, on average, 269. Students whose parents graduated college scored, on average, 299—proficient. Overall, wealthier more advantaged students did better.
- Fourth-Grade Mathematics: Proficiency required a scaled score of 242. The average scaled score for schools with 0–25 percent poverty was 255—proficient. The average scaled score for schools with 76–100 percent poverty was 226. Schools with wealthier students did better.
- Eighth-Grade Mathematics: Proficiency required a scaled score of 299: The average scaled score for schools with 0–25 percent poverty was 299—proficient. The average scaled score for schools with 76–100 percent poverty was 264. Again, schools with wealthier students did better.
- Twelfth-Grade Mathematics: The average scaled score for schools with 0–25 percent poverty was 166. The average scored for schools with 76–100 percent poverty was 130. Again, schools with wealthier students did better.

- *Student Retention Rate*
  - Schools with a low percentage of students eligible for free/reduced lunch (0–25 percent) had a much higher retention rate than schools with a larger percentage of eligible students (76–100 percent). The difference was 60.2 percent retention vs. 5.6 percent retention. Because free/reduced lunch eligibility is a wealth variable, we can see that schools with more wealthy students (i.e., where there are fewer students qualifying for assistance), did better.
  - Suburban schools had a retention rate twice as good as city schools. Suburban schools generally have a wealthier student body.

- *Concentration of Poverty*
  - 38 percent of suburban schools had 0–25 percent students in poverty. That is, almost 40 percent of suburban schools had very few students of poverty.
  - 33.4 percent of city schools had 76–100 percent students in poverty. Whereas about a third of urban schools had many students of poverty.

- *Characteristics of Students*
  - Of all students in the United States, 67.1 percent came from a two-parent household.
  - Of all students in the United States, 24.3 percent came from a mother-only household.
  - Of all the students in the United States, 20.7 percent were living in poverty.

Summary: If poverty and opportunity matter, then the solution to improving achievement would logically be to address these issues, not sanction schools, close them, fire teachers, and/or remove principals.

POVERTY DOES MATTER

Contrary to popular opinion, the achievement data reports are clear—poverty does matter. The Nation's Report Card (NAEP) proves it and those of us who have led urban schools know it to be true. NAEP shows that suburban schools and private schools do better, much better in many cases, than do poorer urban schools. Further, students whose parents graduated from college and who read for fun and who have magazines in the home do better than those who do not.

Pamela A. Cantor, a school turnaround specialist, in a 2010 speech to the Aspen Institute Congressional Education Program, made the link between poverty and poor school performance explicit:

> The problem of underperforming schools is firmly rooted in the relationship between poverty and school failure. The preponderance of the nation's failing schools are located in high poverty urban neighborhoods, communities afflicted by a host of social problems: unemployment, homelessness, substance abuse, community violence, domestic violence, child abuse, teen pregnancy, incarcerated parents, community inefficacy. Students in high poverty communities have a disproportionate number of serious health, mental health and behavioral problems; high poverty families often lack the social capital to advocate for their children; and poor urban neighborhoods lack adequate resources to address the profound level of need.[13]

Cantor's proposed solution, among many recommendations, is to work on improving school culture and to get the needed services to students as part of a school turnaround strategy—an issue we tackle in a following chapter. But the challenges are deeper and are steeped in what schools are tasked to do on a daily basis and what it will take to free them up to be more creative. At the very least, we need to understand that poverty matters—that it negatively impacts children's lives and has a direct relationship to their achievement.

This is not to say that schools should be completely let off the hook for addressing these challenges, but popular turnaround strategies, such as creating more charter and magnet schools and the like, will only impact a small percentage of schools and children nationally. If we want to improve achievement across the board for needy children, we need a national policy to address poverty. Teachers have no control over the social economic status of their students or the nature of their neighborhoods. How, then, can evaluation systems compare districts and teachers when educators have no direct control over the context in which children live that have such a powerful influence on academic achievement?

Joel Klein, the recent chancellor of the New York City Schools in a *Wall Street Journal* op-ed agrees that poverty matters but argues that a good education is the path to ending poverty (rather than focusing on ending poverty to improve education). He cites recent achievement results showing that city charter schools are doing better overall than other schools in high-poverty areas. He states:

> During the eight years I served as chancellor of New York City's public schools, the naysayers and the apologists for the status quo kept telling me "we'll never fix education in America until we fix poverty. I always thought they had it backward, that "we'll never fix poverty until we fix education." Let me be clear. Poverty matters: Its debilitating psychological and physical effects often make it much harder to successfully educate kids who grow up in challenged environments. And we should do everything we can to ameliorate the effects of poverty by giving kids and families the support they need. But that said, I remain convinced that the best cure for poverty is a good education."[14]

We couldn't agree more with Mr. Klein. But as superintendents we would love to have enjoyed the freedoms to be as creative and innovative as are charter schools when it comes to designing programming, allotting resources, improving staff, providing longer school days and . . . the list goes on. In addition, parents who select a charter school may value education more than those parents who do not or who are not as responsible concerning a child's health, education or welfare. Essentially the charter schools that Mr. Klein touts are a form of deregulated public schools under a different name. But even Mr. Klein's numbers demonstrate that charter schools will not be the overall solution for the other 90 to 95 percent of schools in the country. As he notes:

> New York Mayor Michael Bloomberg has opened well over 100 charter schools during his tenure, mostly in high-poverty communities. The response has been overwhelming. This spring, for example, some 67,000 kids applied for fewer than 15,000 openings in charters.

There are over seventeen hundred schools in New York City. The answer, if there truly is one, is to deregulate the rest of them too. And they need more resources to provide supports to close student preparation gaps.

Peter Edelman in a *New York Times* op-ed asks if poverty can be overcome in America and cites four reasons why, for all our efforts, we have not been more successful. He writes:

> An astonishing number of people work at low-wage jobs. Plus, many more households are headed now by a single parent, making it difficult for them to earn a living income from jobs that are typically available. The near disappearance of cash assistance for low-income mothers and children—i.e., welfare—in much of the country plays a contributing role, too. And persistent issues of race and gender mean higher poverty among minorities and families headed by single mothers.[15]

To address poverty Edelman states, "The first thing needed if we're to get people out of poverty is more jobs that pay decent wages. There aren't enough of these in our current economy." Solving that problem, which has persisted for the past forty years, as he notes, is a matter of broad-based federal and state policies, not just of educational effectiveness in the public schools.

The Nation's Report Card clearly shows that over the past twenty to thirty years poverty and poor achievement are closely related. We can close the preparation gap even if we cannot immediately close the poverty gap. And doing so will have a positive impact on achievement.

Further, The Nation's Report Card shows that while some schools do perform poorly, many do quite well. Why then should we apply the same fixes to all schools? Or said another way, why do states and the federal government treat all schools the same?

While it is true that in terms of sanctions and rewards many states reward schools that do well, our judgment is that these rewards are little more than minor efforts when compared to the plethora of regulation and implicit sanctions schools deal with, even good schools, in working within the system.

To put this in perspective, if one of your children had an illness, would you give all your kids the medication prescribed for the one? Does the CEO of GE or IBM or any other large firm apply the same fixes to divisions that are healthy and profitable as those underperforming? Of course not. Then why do we apply the same rules to all public schools?

The fact is that in some cases we do not! Private schools are free from most of the regulatory controls that govern public school life and programming. And the public forms of experimentation with deregulation, namely charter schools, are similarly allowed some, but not all, of the regulatory relief that private schools enjoy. The facts make the point: in the Nation's Report Card private schools do much better on achievement tests than do public schools!

But private and charter schools will not likely serve the masses. At best, it is thought they will serve 5 to 10 percent of the population, so what should be done with the vast majority of schools? And there are data from the Stanford study that charter schools are not the panacea the media make them out to be.[16] Clearly the vast array of reforms and regulations put in place over the past ten to twenty years has not worked, as demonstrated in the Nation's Report Card. We need a different approach, and in this book we call for serious efforts to deregulate public education for that other 90 percent of schools.

SUMMARY

How does the expression go? . . . "Liars figure and figures lie"? Depending on how data is presented and how comprehensive it is, one can draw a very incomplete and often misleading conclusion. The purpose of this chapter has been to demonstrate that we need to look deeper for truth beyond the typical data representations provided in the press, and secondly, that once we do look deeper, we find that not all schools are failing—in fact, many are doing very well. And most of those that are not doing well are trying to catch up for the significant preparation gaps of their students. We do acknowledge that not all failing schools are the result of the preparation gap and that there is a need for changes in these cases, but it is unfair to paint all schools with the same broad brush of failure as is commonly done.

In his book *Proofiness: The Dark Arts of Mathematical Deception*, Charles Seife shows us how data can be manipulated to mislead.[17] Here are a few points he makes that are particularly relevant to school achievement data.

Potemkin numbers: "Potemkin numbers are the mathematical equivalent of Potemkin villages. They're numerical façades that look like real data. Meaningful real-world numbers are tied to a reasonably solid measurement of some sort, at least implicitly. Potemkin numbers aren't meaningful because either they are born out of a nonsensical measurement or they're not tied to a genuine measurement at all, springing forth fully formed from a fabricator's head."[18]

Earlier we discussed reliability and validity as the cornerstones of sound measurement science. When we say that a school had a failing average reading score we assume that the students in this school cannot read. That is simply not the case. Some may not be able to read at the predetermined cutoff score of proficiency, but many do much better. The average is misleading. Moreover, even the failing students can read, just not as well or what the test makers consider to be important.

As an example of this last point, in Streifer's last district, he was concerned that students were not doing well on a specialized elementary reading test. The test included sections on reading comprehension and fluency and combined these two concepts for a total score. When he and the director of instruction interviewed elementary teachers across the district they found that many teachers, perhaps as many as half, just did not believe that fluency should count when determining if a student can read and thus did not spend time with it or scored it improperly on this test. In this example, students "could read" if we believed that comprehension mattered above fluency. As a result, the entire utility of this test is thrown into question. The resulting scores or "numbers" had no basis in reality.

Disestimation: "Disestimation is the act of taking a number too literally, understating or ignoring the uncertainties that surround it. Disestimation imbues a number with more precision than it deserves, dressing a measurement up as absolute fact instead of presenting it as the error-prone estimate that it really is. It's a subtle form of proofiness: it makes a number look more truthful than it actually is."[19]

When we see in the newspaper that the local school has failed, as is often the headline, or that it missed proficiency by 2 points, these are examples of disestimation. Achievement and proficiency are complex topics that just cannot be boiled down to one number. In fact, schooling cannot be boiled down to such a simplicity.

Cherry picking: Cherry picking is the careful selection of data, choosing those that support the argument you wish to make while underplaying or ignoring data that undermine it.[20]

We have seen in The Nation's Report Card (NAEP) how, in fact, so many schools across the country are doing well, especially those that do not have large concentrations of students in poverty. Reporting that America's schools are failing based on NAEP is an example of cherry picking. It just isn't so.

Presenting what students do know is an extremely complex task that does not lend itself to box score representations. Moreover, even if the numbers are sound, the inferences we make from the numbers can only be based around those concepts for which the test was designed. We make the case in this chapter that schooling is much more than just a test score. Finally, even if one wanted to boil schooling down to a test score, that is just not possible given the complex psychometrics involved.

NOTES

1. David Berliner and Bruce Biddle, *The Manufactured Crisis* (Reading, MA: Addison-Wesley, 1995).

2. James W. Popham, *The Truth about Testing: An Educator's Call to Action* (Alexandria, VA: Association for Supervision and Curriculum Development, 2001).

3. James W. Popham, *Everything School Leaders Need to Know about Assessment* (Thousand Oaks, CA: Corwin, 2010).

4. U.S. Department of Education, *The Condition of Education* (Washington, DC: U.S. Government Printing Office, 2012), http://nces.ed.gov/pubsearch/pubsinfo.asp?pubid=2012045

5. Sam Dilllon, "Obama to Seek Sweeping Change in 'No Child' Law," *New York Times*, January 31, 2010. "Overriding a Key Education Law," *New York Times* August 8, 2011.

6. See Sharon Lynn Nichols and David Berliner, *Collateral Damage: How High-Stakes Testing Corrupts America's Schools* (Cambridge, MA: Harvard Education Press, 2007).

7. "The Education of Michelle Rhee," *Frontline*, PBS, January 8, 2013, www.pbs.org/wgbh/pages/frontline/education-of-michelle-rhee/

8. Daniel Pink, *Drive: The Surprising Truth about What Motivates Us* (New York: Riverhead Books, 2009).

9. Mathew Springer, "Accountability Incentives: Do Schools Practice Educational Triage?" *EducationNext* 8, no. 1 (Winter 2008) http://educationnext.org/accountability-incentives/

10. Popham, *The Truth about Testing*, 12.

11. David Denby, "Public Defender: Diane Ravitch Takes On a Movement," *New Yorker*, November 19, 2012, www.newyorker.com/reporting/2012/11/19/121119fa_fact_denby

12. U.S. Department of Education, *The Condition of Education*. The information that follows summarizes the 2012 Condition of Education report. The report is a very robust and comprehensive set of findings that is published annually. It not only indicates how well various groups of students did on the 2012 test but also includes previous years' results so that comparisons can be made over time. To make reading this easier we contemplated creating a summary chart that would have compressed these findings but decided not to do so because that would require violating fundamental psychometrics. For example, just as a schoolwide average for reading is unfair and a more granular approach is necessary to see how students spread along the score range by using standard deviation, it would be wrong for us to compress data here. If we were to combine reading across all grade levels for this section of the chapter based on NAEP and somehow were to collapse the percent who were proficient across many grade levels to make it easier to read, we would be exacerbating that problem. Therefore, what we present is a summary, subject area by subject area, subgroup by subgroup. By reading the entire set of findings in this way it will become apparent which students do well and which do not.

13. Pamela A. Cantor, Deborah S. Smolover, and Joan K. Stamler, "Innovative Designs for Persistently Low-Performing Schools: Transforming Failing Schools by Addressing Poverty-Related Barriers to Teaching and Learning." Turnaround for Children, Inc. www.turnaroundusa.org

14. Joel Klein, "New York's Charter Schools Get an A+: The Success Schools Are Performing at the Same Level as NYC's Gifted and Talented Schools That Select Kids Based Solely on Rigorous Tests," *Wall Street Journal*, July 26, 2012.

15. Peter Edelman, "Poverty in America: Why Can't We End It?" *New York Times*, July 29, 2012.

16. M. Carnoy and R. Rothstein, *What Do International Tests Really Show about U.S. Student Performance?* (Washington, DC: Economic Policy Institute, 2003), www.epi.org/publication/us-student-performance-testing/

17. Charles Seife, *Proofiness: The Dark Arts of Mathematical Deception* (New York: Viking, 2010).

18. Seife, *Proofiness*, Kindle Edition Locations 209–212).

19. (Seife, *Proofiness*, Kindle Edition Locations 300–303).

20. (Seife, *Proofiness*, Kindle Edition Locations 209–212).

Chapter Six

Context, Complexity, and "Complicatedness"

Complexity, which is prevalent in nature and social systems, can inspire complicated and convoluted initiatives. Our past history demonstrates our penchant to turn complex issues into complicated muddles.

Remember the Wall Street whiz kids—the so-called masters of the universe? They were the ones that created complicated derivatives, the impact of which few really understood. The assumption, of course, was that the complex universe of finance could be mastered through ever more complicated investments supported by metrical data and confounding algorithms. Few individuals questioned this approach because it seemed so scientific. Can the data and algorithms and simulations be wrong? Doesn't the universe operate with linear precision like a machine? And, Albert Einstein said, "The most incomprehensible thing about the universe is that it is comprehensible."

Walter Lippmann, the renowned columnist/philosopher, identified a serious problem in examining issues: "We are all captives of the pictures in our head—our belief that the world we have experienced is the world that really exists."[1] In essence our mindscape affects the way we see the world and leadership, raising the questions: What is the natural order of the universe? Is it equilibrium or disequilibrium? Complex or linear? Rigid or adaptive? Machinelike or organic? While these questions seem abstractly philosophical, they are very pragmatic in how we approach life and our work in social systems.

Some take a Newtonian worldview and believe that organizations operate like clockworks. This world is rational and will succumb to analysis and part-to-whole thinking. Gears interact with other gears and produce cause-and-effect action. Linearity and control are the keys. Each mechanism has a role that will be carried out just as designed. Surprises are negative because it throws the "system" off. The designers of No Child Left Behind thought that all we have to do to improve schools is demand higher levels of achievement by testing outcomes and calling underperforming schools failures. Then the system would magically fix itself through standardized test metrics as indicators of education level and competence defined by annual yearly progress.

To others, disequilibrium is reality. The unexpected occurs, ambiguity is in the air, and things seem to be on the verge of being out of control and chaos. "Unknowability" of the future is evident as unexpected issues arise and unseen forces seem to be at work. In this perspective, relationships are critical and the ability to perceive patterns is essential. Rationality does not always rule, but thought is a system that can influence behavior and outcomes. If linear rationality rules, then everything in the world succumbs to the certainty of mathematical models and blueprints. But if disequilibrium is the natural state, then they fall short and we say "that's life."

Nassim Nicholas Taleb, in his book *The Black Swan*, states, "The inability to predict outliers implies the inability to predict the course of history, given the share of these events and the dynamics of events. But we act as though we are able to predict historical events, or, even worse, as if we were able to change the course of history. We produce thirty-year projections of Social Security deficits and oil prices without realizing that we cannot even predict these for next summer—our cumulative prediction errors for political and economic events are so monstrous that every time I look at the empirical record I have to pinch myself to verify that I am not dreaming. What is surprising is not the magnitude of our forecast errors, but our absence of awareness of it."[2]

Our view of the world rubs up against the nonrational context in which public schools and organizations exist. On some planes, rational, linear, cause-and-effect approaches work, particularly in routine day-to-day tasks and operations like changing a tire or troubleshooting a computer malfunction. But in the greater context, sometimes all hell seems to break loose, with demands, expectations, conflict, and requirements coming from all sides and sectors, and immeasurable and subtle forces affecting human behavior. That's what happened with virtually all educational reforms over the past thirty years or so. From *A Nation at Risk* to "Goals 2000" to No Child Left Behind, none have worked very well. Social systems, complex systems, and human beings experience forces and respond emotionally and, sometimes, nonrationally. That's why "the best laid plans" fail and unintended consequences happen.

Public education exists in a complex context as issues explode around the very purpose of education, how it should be organized, and what type of leadership is necessary to make schools successful. In addition to those organizational dynamics, relationship issues bubble up because people bring their unique talent, background, attitude, worldview, and perceptions to their work. While some of these matters can be plotted analytically in designing an organization, creating roles, and defining processes, rationality does not always rule the day because working with people in a dynamic context opens the door to ambiguity, uncertainty, and conflict, along with emotions and rational and "nonrational" tendencies. David Brooks, in a commentary in the *New York Times* on big data stated, "If you adapt a mind-set that replaces the narrative with the empirical, you have problems thinking about personal responsibility and morality, which are based on causation."[3]

AN EDUCATED PERSON

Defining an educated person is more complex than it appears to be. To some, education is essential to developing a civilized and cultivated society that stands on high principles, ethics, and morals. In this context the educational program emphasizes the development of academic skills along with physical, mental, cultural, and social development. In a sense, this is a classic approach that highlights the love of learning and long-term individual character development based on strong values and principles.

A Harvard University symposium sponsored by Harvard's Advanced Leadership Initiative (ALI) defined educated people as those who have "a deep understanding of themselves and how they fit into the world, and have learned what some might call 'soft' skills—complex problem-solving, creativity, entrepreneurship, the ability to manage themselves, and the ability to be life long learners."[4] Participating in the symposium was Deborah DeLisle, of the U.S. Department of Education. She pointed out that "educators often lose sight of creating well-rounded students because they are busy fighting over accountability and who is at fault in the classroom. Then, educators tend to focus on 'silver bullets' and 'best practices' as a means of solving education problems."

The purpose of education has several definitions. Thomas Jefferson believed that a democratic society would not stand unless the citizenry is educated. In this case, the purpose of education is to create informed and involved citizens who are able to analyze issues, evaluate options, and make wise decisions that are in the interests of the common good and not simply based on self-interest. Students would not only be well educated in basic academics, but also in the responsibilities and values that enable them to contribute to a participatory democracy. The bottom line in this context: an educated citizenry equals a vibrant, healthy, and dynamic democracy and culture.

When the economic context sours, the target of the national education agenda seems to shift to the nation's schools as it has most recently with the Great Recession of 2008, as well as other economic downturns. The focus here is on whether the public schools are preparing children for a changing workplace and economy. Schools have been blamed, in part, for unemployment because employers and politicians indicate that they have been unsuccessful in developing intelligent workers who have the academic skills to be trained for a contemporary workforce. Consequently, many employers and politicians see the mission of public schools to supply a workforce to the private and public sectors in a market-driven, competitive economy. The emphasis in this context is placed on skills to ease training for jobs, particularly math and science, as well as reading, technical literacy, and science geared for employment. Hence, the emphasis on STEM: science, technology, engineering, and mathematics.

In addition to the purpose of education, there is the question of defining the desirable outcomes of education. While people debate the purposes, there is also dissonance about the outcomes. Outcomes differ depending upon what the purpose and definition of education is and what qualities a person should have after completing an elementary and secondary education. Textbox 6.1 is a list of the range of outcomes people desire when they debate educational reform.[5]

All of these potential outcomes have some virtue and may meet a particular need or perspective. The outcomes are diverse and come from a variety of sources and interests. Most of these desired outcomes are very difficult to assess metrically through multiple-choice tests or other instruments. Many are qualitative issues that can only be evaluated in retrospect over time, because impacts on the attitudes and values of people take time to mature, for example, character, wisdom, respect, and creativity.

The key question is: can schools and teachers meet all of these expected outcomes in the time and resources at hand? The various reform proposals of the past fifty-plus years makes clear that the federal government emphasis has changed from personal development in the 1950s–1960s, to science/mathematics in the 1970s–1980s, and employment and science, math, engineering, and technical skills in the 1990s–2000s.

Outcomes directly affect accountability: some are tangible and easily measured, and others are not and cannot be quantified metrically or in the present time. Not all outcomes are immediate; they will only be evident with the passage of time as children grow and mature. Some may argue that the most important outcomes are immune to metrical measurement, for example, happiness, good citizenship, fulfillment, creativity, and wisdom. Others advocate for the concrete and measurable, such as rudimentary arithmetic and reading skills.

WHAT GETS MEASURED, GETS . . .

The management guru Peter Drucker asserted, "What gets measured, gets done,"[6] which is the harbinger of dysfunctions as individuals manipulate

> **TEXTBOX 6-1 LIST OF EDUCATIONAL OUTCOMES**
>
> - Acquisition of information about the past and present: includes traditional disciplines such as literature, history, science, mathematics
> - Formation of healthy social and/or formal relationships among and between students, teachers, others
> - Capacity/ability to evaluate information and to predict future outcomes (decision making)
> - Capacity/ability to seek out alternative solutions and evaluate them (problem solving)
> - Development of mental and physical skills: motor, thinking, communication, social, aesthetic
> - Knowledge of moral practices and ethical standards acceptable by society/culture
> - Capacity/ability to recognize and evaluate different points of view
> - Respect: giving and receiving recognition as human beings
> - Indoctrination into the culture
> - Capacity/ability to live a fulfilling life
> - Capacity/ability to earn a living: career education
> - Sense of well-being: mental and physical health
> - Capacity/ability to be a good citizen
> - Capacity/ability to think creatively
> - Cultural appreciation: art, music, humanities
> - Understanding of human relations and motivations
> - Acquisition/clarification of values related to the physical environment
> - Acquisition/clarification of personal values
> - Self-realization/self-reflection: awareness of one's abilities and goals
> - Self-esteem/self-efficacy
>
> *Taken from: www.teachersmind.com/index.html*

measurements, particularly if they are tied to performance evaluation. Today, specific, measurable outcomes, along with data collection, drive the curricular and instructional program, not vice versa. According to some, install a measurable accountability and evaluation system and people will follow. Philosophical debates evaporate. Metrics limit conversation and cause people to "get with it" if they want to keep their jobs. Washington, D.C., is testament to that. Accountability based on tests and other statistics is the hub around which the federal and state education reforms revolve. It raises the issue about what drives the nature of schools as organizations and the definition of education itself.

Are schools nurturing sanctuaries for children to learn, grow and develop their knowledge, skills, attitudes, and physical abilities? Or are they government bureaucracies, complete with a myriad of departments, rules and regulations, and procedures governed by elected state, federal, and local officials? If we want the former, can the straitjacket of complicated and overregulation of the latter even permit such goals to ever be realized?

Reformers faced with rigid bureaucracies and labor contract regulations typically say that the answer to better schools is "competition" and command and control structures. In this mind-set, the market will solve poor-performing schools if parents have a choice. Hence, the push for vouchers, choice, and charter schools.

Vouchers are another issue. In Wisconsin vouchers have not been the panacea advocates thought. The Center on Education Policy (CEP) reviewed a decade of voucher research and finds no clear positive impact on student academic achievement and "mixed outcomes overall for students who attend private schools using vouchers."[7] The report reviews and synthesizes major voucher studies of the past decade. "Overall, several of the most prominent voucher studies released since 2000 conclude that achievement gains for students receiving publicly funded vouchers are similar to those for comparable public school students. These studies include findings from voucher programs in Cleveland, Milwaukee, and Washington, D.C."

"We have a great body of research about the effects of vouchers that policy makers should draw on to inform current debates," said Alexandra Usher, coauthor of the CEP study. "Before state legislators and Congress move quickly to enact new voucher programs, they should consider the evidence from programs already in place for several years to ensure they understand the impacts their policies would have." She added that many voucher studies of the past decade have been sponsored or conducted by organizations with clear positions or mission statements in favor of vouchers. The CEP report also recommends steps to ensure that voucher studies are designed, conducted, and reported in an objective and rigorous way. "We were surprised to find so many studies done by pro-voucher groups," said Nancy Kober, coauthor of the CEP study. "While this doesn't mean researchers with definite positions on vouchers can't be objective, it speaks to the need for outside scrutiny of study methods and guidance from objective expert panels."

The debate about public education misses a critical issue. Are students being well educated or well schooled? There's a difference: one that is seminal in determining almost every other discussion about public education. There is also a difference between education and training. Passing a standardized test is not synonymous with being educated. Many people with prestigious degrees on their walls lack the character, principles, and culture to make selfless and wise decisions.

Behind charter and voucher approaches is the assumption that parents in a competitive education marketplace will make rational decisions and consequently choice will raise all "ships" in the competitive harbor. The erroneous supposition is that public schools are not presently in a competitive market, when in fact local communities understand the impact schools have on community property values, businesses, and standing.

What we do know is that overregulated organizations are not innovative or creative. If data sells, then getting the numbers or the appearance of success based on data become important, even if the numbers are exaggerated and misleading. People stay trapped thinking within the box and do not take the risk of failure or fear of sanctions or punishment.

Gary Rubenstein, a school reformer for fifteen years and proponent of Teach for America (TFA), takes issue with the metrical data used to promote charter schools and the reform movement. In a *New York Times* article, he is quoted as saying that standardized test scores may seem "like a good idea in theory" but he believes test scores are too imprecise and subject to "random variation" to be used for teacher ratings and hiring and firing decisions.[8] Rubenstein has been close to the TFA reform movement and indicated that many charter schools' data on student test scores and graduation rates didn't measure up to what the schools claimed. In one charter school he cites, the claim of a high graduation rate didn't take into account a high attrition rate. The class started with seventy-three tenth graders and dwindled to forty-four seniors. Many of those who left returned to public schools because their needs couldn't be met in the charter.

Today, Drucker's statement about measurement and accomplishment has been reduced to quantifiable metrics in the guise of standardized tests. Schools are vested in "data-based decision making" emulating their perception of how business operates. Relationships, however, are difficult to quantify and are frequently seen as "soft" as compared to hard numbers that drop out of spreadsheets and so-called data banks.

In New York City, the release of test data tied to teacher evaluations created a firestorm because some of the data were inaccurate and demonstrated some validity problems about teacher performance from year to year. In other words, the records were poorly maintained and the tests themselves were problematic. Teachers' unions and others have responded to the test fetish. Ravitch states, "the Committee on Appropriate Test Use of the National Research Council stated in an authoritative report in 1999 that 'tests are not perfect' and a test score is not an exact measure of the students knowledge or skills."[9] Unfortunately this test fetish has morphed into teacher assessment as discussed in the previous chapter.

The debate about outcomes has revolved around the locus of control for America's schools. But no matter where the locus of control of education rests, measurable accountability is the norm, and in this context, even principals, teachers, and parents are beginning to rise up against our nation's obsession with standardized testing. The Florida unit of the National Education Association,[10] in April 2013, filed a lawsuit against the state department, contending that the formula used to assess teachers violates their constitutional rights. More cases in other states are expected to be filed on this issue across the country.

Determining the purpose of education, the nature of the school organization and how to measure its effectiveness is a critical debate that goes directly to the leadership and management of public schools. Schools cannot be all things to all people nor should assessment and accountability systems be so limited that they drive schools to simplistic, narrow organizations that exclude essential outcomes necessary for the success of our country in a complex global, social, and economic context. Should what is easily measured dictate what outcomes we desire in determining what is important in educating our children?

ATTITUDE, THOUGHT, AND SYSTEMS

The mind frame of reformers who perceive education as achievement on tests limits creative and innovative teachers and schools. Our mind frames directly affect our actions about education and what we think leaders and teachers control. Basically, leaders directly control few but very important things.

Certainly, how and what leaders think about is in their total control and purview. The physicist David Bohm stated that thought is a system and collective thought is a powerful force that can influence what emerges and gets accomplished.[11] When we discuss systems, we forget that thought itself is a system that can powerfully influence behavior and attitudes.

We usually think that systems only include tangible components. Bohm, however, warns about the problem of fragmentation. He believes that systems thinking views organizations as interconnected, dynamic, and evolving. Fragmented thinking, however, creates separation and results in conflict and failures. Just looking at parts or processes in isolation can be destructive and can produce dramatic unanticipated consequences. So thinking is important, and in some cases, more important than rushing to "doing" something.

Leaders also control their attitudes—some are optimists and some are pessimists. Our attitude and how we think certainly affects our behavior and our relationships that are critical in creating organizations that encourage people to fulfill themselves in their work. Fulfillment means that they use their skills and talents to the maximum, and simultaneously find satisfaction and efficacy in their work. Motivation and commitment come from these opportunities, not from coercive power.

UNCONTROLLABLES

Educational leaders, however, already faced with many "uncontrollables" in the form of regulations, mandates, rulings, and laws are also dealing with "uncontrollable" external factors. The world and national economy, for example, is not the province of local school leaders or even under the direct control of the president of the United States. Despite mathematical formulas and strategic initiatives, the economy responds to the ethereal force of consumer confidence. But research shows and we demonstrated in a previous chapter that poverty has an impact on children's health and welfare, including their educational performance.

Global competition and trade have dramatically altered the employment picture in the United States. Technology brought unheard-of changes from just a few years ago. Demographics and birth rate are beyond local control. Family structures have changed and the dynamics are beyond the control of educators. All of these and more are factors in complex systems.

In addition, innovations changed the landscape. The technological advances that have occurred over the past thirty years have been monumental. Taleb stated, "When I asked people to name three recently implemented technologies that most impact our world today, they usually propose the computer, the Internet, and the laser. All three were unplanned, unpredicted, and unappreciated upon their discovery."[12] But those technologies have changed the world, including how we can educate children.

All of the "uncontrollables" in the greater context of schools are extremely significant: the locus of power, the nature of communication, national and state priorities, the nature of how children learn, the family structure and support, the structure of organizations, the impact of international competition and conflict, and the many other facets of our personal or public lives.

School leaders have to work in this dynamic environment. The complex context is challenging and continually changing. It is filled with a multitude of diverse demands and expectations, many of them incongruent. Leaders today require sophisticated competencies to lead successfully in this context and the freedom to exercise imaginative judgment, creativity, and innovation. Unfortunately, that freedom is lacking in many cases due to the straitjacket of overregulation. Artistry falls victim to standardization and regulation.

EXPECTATIONS AND PRESSURE

Expectations also emanate from different sources, including leaders themselves for their own performance and aspirations. Meeting their own expectations can create intense pressure and stress, particularly since the environment in which they work is so volatile and sometimes "nonrational."

Other expectations come from the external context and sources, many of them based on self-interest, not the common good. The expectations these groups have may be opposed—and contradictory—resulting in conflict. Pleasing everyone and meeting everyone's expectations is a goal without a solution, plausibility, or success. It is not possible.

In this circumstance, building credibility is essential for a leader. But the conflict of multiple expectations is haunting and daunting. Major leadership issues concern integrity and credibility in leading through difficult and confounding educational and economic challenges.

Leadership rests on credibility, and credibility rests on truth. Telling the truth may not be popular but it is the right thing to do. Leaders with moral courage do not tell people what they want to hear, but what they need to know. In a political, social, and economic environment, leaders have to engage the community in a conversation about the schools so that the conflict of multiple expectations does not explode into dysfunction and demagogic factions. Doing so requires leaders who are genuine and principled in their behavior and who listen and create a dialogue around the goals of the schools.

Political pressure on school leaders today is great. There is the expectation to show measurable progress of the school system, individual schools, and teachers. It takes courage for leaders to discuss some of the issues that are not within their control that affect learning. Parent expectations, the state of students' home life, the economic condition of the community, and the local political discourse on funding other issues requires the moral courage to engage in the conversation.

The personal risks are great. Individual leaders who speak out directly risk their jobs because they may alienate school board members and other powerful community leaders of a particular political disposition and incur the rancor of community groups. The social, political, and economic pressures in a local community are immense and require individuals with strong ethics and principles to stand up and lead and to do more than simply manage the system.

The complexity of leading a multifaceted organization like a school system is challenging. All of the structural components of the organization are interconnected and react in unified as well as discrete ways. Organizations are not engines. They are guided through values, intuition, and constructive relationships between people and groups, as well as data and information.

In addition to the pressure of multiple expectations and high performance, there is also the weight and pressure of standardization and uniformity. Standards, along with uniform accountability, place pressure on organizations from several standpoints.

The call for standardized results *and* processes from the state and federal governments places demands and controls on schools that curtail locally developed priorities and programs that meet local needs. Standards and mandates can shackle local initiatives and exhaust the limited resources of time and finances. Creativity and initiative are the victims of standardization, as are the customization of educational programs for children.

Standardized processes may work for making cars or pharmaceuticals, but standards are often mediocre and ineffective in addressing the unique needs of students whose progress cannot always be measured in fixed time frames or through regimented approaches. Intellectual, emotional, and physical maturity are different for each child, as are the emotional and physical health and disposition. A multitude of striking examples exist of highly creative people who were not perceived to be effective in school, for example:

- Teachers told Thomas Edison he was "too stupid to learn anything."
- Orville and Wilbur Wright battled depression and family illness before starting the bicycle shop that led them to experimenting with flight.
- Winston Churchill struggled and failed the sixth grade.
- The testing director of MGM noted that Fred Astaire, "Can't act. Can't sing. Slightly bald. Can dance a little."
- Robin Williams suffered from attention deficit disorder.
- Walt Disney was fired by a newspaper editor because he lacked "imagination and good ideas."
- Albert Einstein did not speak until he was four and did not read until he was seven. His teachers thought he was mentally handicapped.
- Emily Dickinson was reclusive and all but ignored having fewer than a dozen poems published out of her 1,800 completed works.

Metrical standards can place local school leaders in awkward positions because they do not take into account the individual district's nature, norms, socioeconomic profile, or resources. The data on NAEP demonstrate that the needs of poor and urban children are different and may require approaches and time frames distinct from their middle-class and suburban colleagues. All school districts do not face the same environments or challenges. Expecting standardized results in the same time frame when resources and students needs vary is difficult, if not impossible. Meeting standards in different schools may take more time, varied intensity and effort, and varied approaches and methods.

The resources available to schools are limited and subject to greater demands and difficult revenue streams. In a nutshell, demands are up and resources are either the same or declining. Keeping pace with program mandates and requirements with reduced or little funding for them taxes (excuse the pun) local resources. "Producing more with less" is a great slogan if you are making widgets but not when parents expect the best education for their children and "less" means limited opportunity or program reductions. Federal and state mandates are usurping available funds.

In addition to all this, working with changing demographics is a political, economic, and educational reality. Schools run on talent, not technology or equipment. The competition for talented teachers and administrators is brisk. Demographics play a part in the equation of finding talent and in gaining support for schools. The number of senior citizens is growing, and they have priorities that may not be directed toward elementary and secondary education. In addition, people available to fill new positions to replace the growing number of retirees are limited.

Finally, the political context demands candor, integrity, credibility, and courage. Leadership requires that a conversation take place in a community so that a cohesive direction can be set and resources applied. It does not mean that everyone agrees, but it does require that everyone is alert to the issues and that they respect the leadership in presenting the challenges and implementing solutions. It requires more than data manipulation and engineering processes. Leading in a complex system requires dialogue, systems thinking, and strong, respectful relationships.

COMPLEXITY AND COMPLICATIONS

The world seems to move at a breakneck, hectic pace. We seem to be caught trying to keep up and respond to the speed. Technology hasn't helped. In fact it may be a part of the problem, as people react in a Pavlovian mode at meetings, responding to the buzz of their cell phones.

We have mountains of data and hundreds of choices at our disposal that demand a response—right now. We yearn for simpler times, as we seem awash in complexity. In response, we lean on strategic and empirical approaches to find the magic key—the coordinates—that will unlock the secrets to success. We need information. We mine data. We seek certainty. Big data is now all the rage.

In the process, we fragment our world, our problems, and ourselves into an increasing number of categories and pieces. Organizations are replete with "we-they" interactions—we sort people and forces into those with us or those against us. We segment ourselves when our natural inclination is to find togetherness and belonging as we try to find our place in this complex world.

In facing this world, we seek control and predictability in the push for standardization via regulation, rules, policies, union contracts, or the philosophical disposition of those in leadership positions. These attempts at standardizing behavior often lead to complications. The penchant for control through rule-driven behavior results in monitoring, inspecting, and hierarchical procedures, which results in more paperwork, tight line and staff behavior, lost motivation, and increased cynicism. Winston Churchill quipped, "If you have ten thousand regulations, you destroy all respect for the law."

Volatility, uncertainty, and ambiguity are realities that will not go away, raising the question: do things have to be complicated in a complex context? Does simplicity mean oversimplification? But there are solutions besides being shackled to complicated approaches.

Defining principles, beliefs, ethics can create an orderly, innovative, and creative system. Connections based on simple rules, Wheatley maintains, can create complex behavior.[13] For example, she cites two examples of complex, self-regulating behavior. A flock of birds flying in a tight circle change direction without collisions because each bird determines its behavior based on information about what its neighbors are doing. Likewise, traffic flowing into New York with thousands of vehicles of all types traveling to thousands of different destinations takes place because of the simple self-organizing rules of: (1) stay in your lane, (2) maintain your speed, and (3) signal your intention. Can you imagine what regulations the Department of Transportation would require if Congress addressed New York's or any large city's rush hour traffic jams? The regulations would stack seven feet high.

The antidote to complicatedness and overregulation includes:

- Simplicity. Simplify the process by taking away the root causes of the difficulty. Unnecessary paperwork? Eliminate It! Powermongers in the way? Eliminate unnecessary staff, paper, and procedures that are hedgerows to productivity and creativity. Bureaucracy in the way? *Think: flattening the organization.*
- New thinking and perspectives. Complicatedness results because of outmoded thinking disconnected from the realities and changes in the greater

context. Reviewing procedures and adopting new approaches and technologies can simplify work. *Think: digitized photography and the demise of Kodak.*
- Redesign. Bad design can impose arbitrary blocks and limits to completing work. Machines that are poorly designed have extraneous parts and too many operations to be efficient. The same is true of organizational design. Redesigning roles, role relationships, decision-making discretion, and other processes can enhance innovative thinking and satisfaction. *Think: Microsoft and corporate culture.*
- Side effects. Things become complicated because of anxiety about the unknown and the need for control. What occurs is a cycle of complications. No Child Left Behind is an example of reactions to the side effects of the law and its complications. The best thing to do is to stop responding to side effects, thereby eliminating more confusion, anxiety, and new side effects. If not, the result is greater complications. *Think: teaching to the test, the narrow curriculum, and educational triage and the impact on professional ethics.*

Complex systems consist of many autonomous and diverse components that are interrelated and interdependent. The parts of a complex system reflect the whole. Complex systems do not operate like clockworks. They, like many social systems, or human economies, have dynamic and nonlinear interactions. Each component, however, may also be complex, responding to their context in more than one and diverse ways.

Chaos theory establishes that the world does not always respond to step-by-step analysis. Planning for the long term is difficult. Newtonian thinking loses its effect because of the premise that tomorrow is going to be much like today. But we know that doesn't always happen. There are those unexpected events, which sometimes occur from small actions, which alter our lives and world.

Einstein stated, "We cannot solve our problems with the same thinking we used when we created them." Newton may have been right about gravity, but his cause-and-effect world does not really exist in the seemingly nonrational world of quantum mechanics. If he was right, there would be no unexpected consequences, our sequential plans would fire off with perfection, everything that is important would be measurable, and all problems would succumb to rational problem solving through part-to-whole thinking—breaking issues into parts and addressing them separately.

Dee Hock, founder and CEO emeritus of Visa, stated in his book *Birth of the Chaordic Age* that leaders, scientists, and others "seem to be intrigued with the notion that the two-hundred-year-old scientific attempt to explain the universe and all it contains as mechanisms operating with precise, linear laws of cause and effect may be inadequate."[14] Educational reformers are similarly intrigued.

COMPLEXITY

Peter Senge identified two types of complexity: detail complexity and dynamic complexity. Detail complexity concerns managing many variables through sophisticated tools of forecasting, business analysis, and strategic plans. It concerns cause-and-effect chains of data, processes, and mathematical simulations. Assembling a machine like an automobile involves detail complexity and clear cause-and-effect directions. Managing inventory also involves detail complexity. Following directions or a recipe has a clear and direct impact in these situations.

On the other hand, dynamic complexity involves situations in which cause and effect are subtle and where the impact of interventions is not obvious. With this complexity, the same actions may have different short- or long-term effects. "When an action has one set of consequences locally and a very different set of consequences in another part of a system, there is dynamic complexity. When obvious interventions produce non-obvious consequences, there is dynamic complexity."[15]

An example in education is the innovation of magnet schools around selected themes and areas of study. However, the impact of that intervention, which was not intended, reduces or depletes student leadership in the remaining general high schools. Quality schools need good student leaders, and with talented motivated students going to magnet schools, student leadership in general high schools was reduced, affecting organizational climate.

Senge goes on to say that "the real leverage in most management situations lies in understanding dynamic complexity, not detailed complexity." We get caught up in details failing to see patterns and finding answers. We look for the silver bullet or recipe that we can follow to construct a new reality. The problem is that that reality is often immune to these approaches and, in fact, produces serious negative unanticipated consequences.

Scapegoating is the residue of a mindscape that views the world through linear cause-and-effect lenses. Reformers and the media have tried to determine the simple cause for children's poor performance. Hence, teachers unions are proclaimed the major cause of poor schools. And, of course, "lousy teachers" are not far behind in the scapegoating game. We have reduced a complex system—the school system—down to a few isolated villains.

Wheatley defined the problem: "In a complex system, it is impossible to find simple causes that explain our problems or know who to blame. A messy tangle of relationships is responsible for these unending crises. . . . We can't make sense of the world using analytical processes we were taught or understand the complexity of modern systems by reductionism."[16]

But what about control? Many leaders feel that they need control so problems can be addressed and progress made. Some coworkers and committee members want a leader to be "the captain" giving them a sense that someone in authority is seemingly in control.

The media, as we have seen, become enchanted with egocentric reformers who run through the schools directing blame, dictating orders, and making evaluations. Power is the answer to some. These images live off the illusion that leaders have total control over the context in which they work. Anyone serving in a leadership position understands that what they control directly can be outflanked by the "uncontrollables" in the organizational or greater context.

Pushing people through coercion is far different from motivating them. It stymies effort and progress. Creating new systems and procedures is one thing, but getting people to use them creatively and ethically is another. Arie deGues points out that "companies die because managers focus on economic activity of producing goods and services, and they forget that their organization's true nature is that of a community of humans."[17] In education we focus on test scores and analytics and forget that schools are social systems, inhabited by teachers, students, and others needs as well as responsibilities.

Absent coercive power what can leaders do to create adaptive and innovative organizations? To begin with, they need to understand the difference between order and control. Wheatley believes that with complex interactive systems with independent components, order, not control, is essential. When people see and understand that they have shared interests and that they need each other, they reach out, work together, and self-organize to get the job done. Think: 9/11. Sharing similar beliefs and values are important. With schools, a shared idea or a common definition of the purpose of education is imperative. Running off in twenty different directions is dysfunctional and counterproductive.

Therefore, there is a need for flexibility with an emphasis on organizational learning. Continually getting feedback and examining our mental models are essential in a world that is not always predictable and rational. Quality leaders push for questioning and challenging and stopping conformity of thought because, as Bohm indicates, thought is a powerful system. Seeing patterns and an openness to "accidents" can lead to insight and success.

SUMMARY

Reinventing the organization so that it can self-organize in the face of ambiguity and uncertainty is essential in dealing with the constant change in schools and other organizations. That change sometimes can only be seen in retrospect because it happens in piecemeal fashion or viewed in isolation of the greater picture. Change can only happen if a dialogue takes place between all parties in a school, not through carrot-and-stick controls. Motivation, not simply power-induced movement, is necessary.

NOTES

1. Jeffrey Kane, *Education, Information, and Transformation: Essays on Learning and Thinking* (New York: Merrill, 1999), 96.

2. Nassim Nicholas Taleb, *The Black Swan* (New York: Random House, 2007), xx.

3. David Brooks, "What You'll Do Next," *New York Times*, April 16, 2013.

4. Harvard Graduate School of Education, Advanced Leadership Initiative, "Defining the Educated Person," Askwith Forums, www.gse.harvard.edu/news-impact/2012/04/watch-the-askwith-forum-live-defining-the-educated-person/

5. Educational Outcomes. Available on Internet: www.teachersmind.com/index.html

6. Drucker quote: Lucid, Brian. "What Gets Measures Gets Done," *ALN Magazine*, Available on Internet: www.alnmagazine.com/article/what-gets-measures-gets--done

7. Alexandra Usher and Nancy Kober, *Keeping Informed about School Vouchers: A Review of Major Developments and Research* (Washington, DC: Center on Education Policy, 2011), www.cep-dc.org/cfcontent_file.cfm?Attachment=Usher_Voucher_072711.pdf

8. Gary Rubenstein, "Teachers and Policy Makers," *New York Times*, January 31, 2013.

9. Ravitch, Diane, *The Death and Life of the Great American School System* (New York: Basic Books, 2010), 153.

10. Stephen Sawchuck, "Florida Unions Sue Over Test-Score Based Evaluation," *Education Week*, April 16, 2013, www.edweek.org/ew/articles/2013/04/16/29lawsuit.h32.html

11. David Bohm, *Thought as a System* (New York: Routledge, 1992).

12. Taleb, *The Black Swan*, 135.

13. Margaret Wheatley, *Finding Our Way: Leadership for an Uncertain Time* (San Francisco, CA: Berrett-Koehler Publishers, 2006), 204–5.

14. Dee Hock, *Birth of the Chaordic Age* (San Francisco, CA: Berrett-Koehler, 1999), 27.

15. Senge, Peter, *The Fifth Discipline* (New York: Currency, 2006), 71.

16. Wheatley, *Finding Our Way*, 101.

17. Ari DeGues, *The Living Company* (Boston: Harvard Business Review Press, 2002), 3. Education Outcomes: www.teachersmind.com/index.html

Chapter Seven

Unshackling Creativity and Innovation

Thomas Hobson (1544–1631) was a livery stable owner in Cambridge, England. To rotate the use of his horses, he offered customers the choice of either taking the horse in the stall nearest the door or taking none at all. A Hobson's choice is a free choice in which only one option is offered. The choice is between taking the option or not: "take it or leave it." The "Race to the Top" is the Hobson's choice of school reform. You can get in the "race" if you ride the education department's horse.

The United States Department of Education's answer to achieving more successful schools emphasizes accountability through a carrot-and-stick approach to motivate school districts and teachers to change. To enter the "race," school districts must submit a proposal meeting preordained strategies/policies (the designated horse) if they want to receive the cash. The so-called motivation is money. If you do not agree with the requirements, you are out of luck—you can't ride. Being creative was not the goal; compliance was.

Second, the Feds want teachers to be evaluated based on "data," which translates into whether or not they have demonstrated value-added progress on the basis of student standardized tests, even though teachers have no control over such critical factors as poverty, student health, family structure, or parent support. In addition, value-added instruments have questionable reliability, according to Stanford's study by Linda Darling-Hammond and Edward Haertel: "First, we found that value-added models of teacher effectiveness are highly unstable. Teachers' ratings differ substantially from class to class and from year to year, as well as from one test to the next."[1]

Ironically, even though the federal reformers espouse data-based approaches and decisions, data about their own reforms focused on school accountability and teacher effectiveness do not reflect sound research. The

Feds fly in the face of a host of research data in these cases. There is a serious gap between what the federal government wants in public schools and what research data indicate. Concerning motivation, the Feds' carrot-and-stick approach contradicts well-established research that goes back decades (see research of Maslow, Herzberg, McGregor, Vroom, McClelland, and Pink).

In addition, the conventional wisdom in Washington is that teachers are the most important influence on student achievement. This is a distortion of the research. The accurate finding is that teachers are the most important "*in-school* influence" concerning students' education. Economic conditions, family instability, emotional issues, and other community factors have a large influence on student attitudes and performance in school. These are beyond the control of teachers and educators and carry a large impact on achievement.

Richard Rothstein states, "Decades of social science research have demonstrated that differences in the quality of schools can explain about one-third of the variation in student achievement. The other two-thirds are attributable to non-school factors."[2] Additionally, he suggests reforms can create a "frozen bureaucracy," producing red tape, excessive measurement and documentation, and change by the "book," which basically means doing it the way bureaucrats mandate. The emphasis is on stability, control, and continuity that lead to standardization not innovation.

The federal rubric for reform works against gifted people entering the profession—facing a bloated bureaucracy, paperwork, and mandates stymies innovative people and results in inconsequential collaborative efforts, if any at all. Assessing teachers, even in part, on assessments of questionable validity and reliability will deter quality people from working in classrooms. Without a sense of control and efficacy, why would creative people want to teach or lead schools? Schools need innovators, not bureaucrats: they require imagination, not unquestioning belief.

CREATIVITY QUALITIES AND KILLERS

Creativity is essential to any enterprise that operates in a dynamic environment. Schools are no exception. As we indicated earlier, they function in the social, political, economic, and organizational context that is constantly evolving. In this environment, creativity is essential for consistent performance over time, as well as survival. Most leaders profess the necessity of creativity but unintentionally kill it by trying to maximize coordination, productivity, and control.

Creativity doesn't happen by getting struck by lightning. Popular culture frequently provides a distorted picture of creative people and organizations.

There are several key components to creativity. Csikszentmihalyi defined creativity as "any act, idea, or product that changes an existing domain, or that transforms an existing domain into a new one."[3] Robinson in the book *Out of Our Minds* agrees and indicates that creativity is a "process of having creative ideas that have value."[4]

Imaginative thinking involves synthesizing ideas into new combinations, which is a high form of complex thinking. Examining with fresh eyes and testing ideas from various areas is the foundation of synthesis. In fact, creativity is more than having an imagination "because it requires that you actually do something rather than lie around thinking about it. It's a very practical process of trying to make something original."[5]

Second, expertise is essential in terms of knowing fundamental concepts and skills in the broad arena of their work. It involves thinking conceptually, mastering content areas, and applying of pertinent skills.[6]

Third, motivation requires the basic ability to persevere on difficult challenges as well as the patience to let ideas incubate. Reflection and trial and error are frequent partners in innovation. Individuals must have desire to do something important and find joy in the challenge and interest in their work.

Basically, strong intrinsic motivation is essential for creativity. High performers are not stymied by failure but instead present a positive outlook and see failure as a false start, a glitch, or a part of the learning process. They have high tolerance for uncertainty and do not fear failing. Children and teachers need to understand that strategic or outcome failure can bring insight and progress. Who can succeed 100 percent of the time?

Within an organization, creativity is not a competitive endeavor because competition can limit or reduce the encouragement for people to work together. Competitive internal cultures have serious problems, as we indicated in the chapter on culture. We frequently think that competition is a solution to any challenge and produces progress and productivity. But it can create a sense of self-consciousness on the part of some workers who worry about the perception of others of their competence and capability. They become hesitant to contribute. For others, this climate curtails sharing and collaboration. The constant expectation of evaluation can undermine individuals' creative spirit and efforts for fear of looking bad in a judgmental setting.

Competition also gets in the way when there is a significant need to work together to solve problems. Looking good becomes more important than being good and becomes the enemy of creating a learning organization. If we feel a need to "look good," it is difficult for us to expose that there are things we do not know or did not accomplish. Competition can result in individuals working in isolation, putting the best face on their efforts and protecting themselves from criticism.

Finally, education is not a race, and America's penchant to turn everything into a competition can actually work against educators finding solutions to complicated problems. A continuous crisis mentality, first of all, is not useful, and secondly, results in focusing blame for difficult issues that have very complex roots. In this climate, success has a thousand mothers and failure has none.

Information is absolutely critical to gain productive insight. Data to be useful needs to be turned into information and used properly. Open systems are more creative because information is shared and exchanged and not accumulated and stored. Getting new insight from these types of connections across the organization and with external sources leads to deeper knowledge and perspective.

Closed systems wear down and squander energy as individuals stand by and watch the system atrophy. The desire for conformity and equilibrium exhausts the capacity for change and dissipates creative energy. Open systems on the other hand engage with the outer environment and continue to grow and evolve. Sometimes things seem chaotic in the sense that disequilibrium exists, which, ironically, is a "necessary condition for a system's growth."[7]

Wheatley also asserts the following: "information = in–formation."[8] Quality information helps people understand issues and align effort. Information creates the pattern around which people can mobilize to address problems skillfully and inventively. Leaders cannot demand creativity and innovation on the spot and at a definite time. Innovation requires autonomy at the local level with the people closest to the issue working together. Self-organizing to share mind-sets and synthesizing ideas can uncover distinctive or new applications and solutions. Information is a big organizer in these situations. Negativity can derail creative and innovative thinking if communication and risk taking are deterred.

Excellence is not a static state that can be produced by following a recipe. Certain organizational conditions are essential for producing a creative culture. These conditions relate to management and leadership that address challenge, freedom, resources, supervision, and organizational support. Each of these categories has positive or negative features that will either promote or stymie creativity.

CHALLENGES AND MOTIVATION

"The good news is that the principal role of a creative leader is not to have all the ideas; it is to nurture a culture where everyone can have new ideas."[9]

Creative people respond to challenges that are important and significant to them. We all want to find meaning in our lives, and many professional people discover it through tackling challenging pursuits at work. Leaders match the right challenge or opportunity with the right people, choosing individuals who have a deep interest in the challenge, and the skills, thinking sophistication, and background, to confront it.

Expertise and ability to think creatively are the raw materials an individual brings to the challenge. Motivation comes from within the person, raising a personal sense of challenge to solve the problem and the satisfaction that comes with it. Extrinsic motivation, better described as enforced movement, is external to the individual and rests on the ability to get something desirable or to avoid something painful. The application of extrinsic motivational methods eventually leads to dysfunctional consequences, which are described later in this chapter.

Facing challenges requires freedom, the autonomy to determine the means and processes to approach the problem. Intrinsically this is motivating because the individual has the ability to act efficaciously in responding to the successes and failures they experience in pursuing the challenge. Autonomy over the means to address the problem is the key to providing intrinsic satisfaction that comes with a clearly articulated challenge.

Amabile and Khaire discuss the role of leadership in developing creative cultures.[10] Leaders can sour an individual's creative juices by not defining the challenge or goal clearly or changing goals throughout the process. Micromanagers kill initiative because they strip the individual of any control in solving the problem, resulting in alienation or passive aggression. In these circumstances, the loss of an individual's initiative results in disaffection.

Supervisory encouragement requires interpersonal and conceptual support of individuals' efforts. Praising the work of people about the project and letting them know that the work matters is motivating. Negativity, cynicism, or skepticism destroys the openness of communication, the quality of divergent thinking, and the sense of motivation. People fear the risk of being openly honest if no one listens or if there are sanctions for doing so.

Failing to acknowledge innovative efforts is severely demoralizing. Leaders with open minds sustain people's passion and develop the positive energy to put forth best efforts and ideas and persevere in difficult times. In many cases, positive energy and words are more powerful than materialistic rewards. Intrinsic motivation is the driving force for people to continue to engage in noble work, even in the face of overwhelming circumstances.

Leaders must also formulate the proper workgroup to take on a challenge. Getting the right people in the room with the knowledge and expertise is important. Putting a team together with distinct backgrounds and including individuals recognized for their talent and knowledge are powerful assets. These teams develop relationships that can produce greater results because individuals with different mind-sets, slants, and ideas inspire creative thought. It may take more time, but it can produce results that are valuable and innovative in accomplishing the organization's goals.

Successful and creative teams need a mix of people with divergent ideas. Having people who think alike and approach problems the same way may produce quicker answers, but not the most creative ones. Divergent thought and approaches coupled in a dialogue process can move groups beyond pedestrian answers and methods. Dialogue of this type can cause participants to see problems and issues with "new eyes."

Finally, creative endeavors require time, money, and organizational support in the form of having appropriate procedures in place so that individuals can share information, ideas, and results. Placing people in organizational cocoons is a deadly practice, even if they do have the resources to operate. Fear and punishment cause people to insulate themselves and not share insights. Loneliness at the top also does not lead to ingenious or visionary leaders. They die in cocoons—isolated from information and people's expertise.

Leaders, who propose fake deadlines or impossibly tight ones, jeopardize the enterprise. Bogus time constraints impair professional performance. Too little time or insufficient fiscal resources curtail the group's efforts and breakthroughs and increase leaders' frustration. Individuals pressed for quick answers can result in shortcuts that can be strategically or ethically questionable as the cases in Washington, D.C., and other areas demonstrate.

An organization's culture must support open conversation and debate about ideas to kindle inventive outcomes. Providing money as a reward to do things a certain way will result in individuals feeling controlled and manipulated. Politicking, gossiping, and infighting are cancers that can spread throughout the effort and stymie any ingenuity and originality. This pettiness is detrimental in program development and research, as well as general operations. People keep their heads down and don't risk or bring attention to them. "It's not my job" is a moniker that spells cultural dysfunction.

In summary, nurturing creativity and passion gives individuals a sense of efficacy because they feel they can make a difference and contribute positively. Allowing time for thought and reflection and allowing individuals to step away, renew themselves, and let their unconscious work on issues can bring insight through the use of left- and right-brain reasoning as well as intuition.

Innovation and creativity are not synonymous. Creativity is the ability to develop the "big" idea, and innovation is the ability to translate the idea into practice. In many cases, it's not a lack of great ideas that causes the demise of organizations but a lack of the ability to implement successfully those ideas and produce better results.

MOTIVATION, NOT MOVEMENT

Motivating people is not running around the halls of the school with a Blackberry in each hand, inspecting, shouting commands, and taking names. Superintendents or principals who think providing an external motivational KITA (kick in the _ _ _, according to Frederick Herzberg[11]) do not comprehend the research data on motivating people to do creative work. Power plays are not very effective and can result in dysfunctional behavior if they are wrapped in the aura of fear and punishment. Egocentric celebrity reformers may garner attention in the media for themselves but can do serious damage. Destruction is much easier and quicker that construction.

Some school reformers propose approaches to motivation that have their roots in the early 1900s in the work of Frederick Winslow Taylor, the father of scientific management. Taylor believed that "It is only through *enforced* standardization of methods, *enforced* adoption of the best implements and working conditions, and *enforced* cooperation that this faster work can be assured. And the duty of enforcing the adoption of standards and enforcing this cooperation rests with *management* alone."[12] Sound familiar?

Taylor wanted to transfer control from workers to management, and he thought that by analyzing work, the "'One Best Way' to do it would be found and then detailed plans specifying the job and how it was to be done could be formulated and communicated to the workers."[13] Research has since challenged and refuted this approach to management and motivation.

Daniel Pink indicates that there is a big breach between what science knows about motivation and what businesses and organizations do.[14] School systems are falling into the same abyss, disregarding powerful data and following organizational mythology. Pink indicates that they are ignoring one of the most robust research findings available concerning motivation—that "if-then" rewards can have the opposite effect of what was intended because they stifle, rather than, stimulate creative thinking.

Secretary of Education Arne Duncan wants the best and brightest to become teachers, all the while advocating a carrot-and-stick approach to evaluating teachers. Pink states, "Carrots and sticks can achieve precisely the opposite of their intended aims. Mechanisms designed to increase motivation can dampen it. Tactics aimed at boosting creativity can reduce it. Programs to promote good deeds can make them disappear. Meanwhile, instead of restraining negative behavior, rewards and punishments can often set it loose—and give rise to cheating, addiction, and dangerously myopic thinking." Thinking "outside the box" is off-limits, as is challenging the status quo. Why take the risk of failure when the "stick" is near?

Many current reforms rest on the unstable foundation of extrinsic control. Bonuses can "move" people, but they do not motivate them. Frederick Herzberg's "One More Time, How Do You Motivate Employees?" pointed this out decades ago.[15] This article sold 1.2 million reprints by 1987 and was the most requested article from the *Harvard Business Review*. Money will *move* people only so far, and then individuals ask for an increase in payment or more frequent payments in order to continue or repeat the same amount of work. More money is required for the same effort.

Movement is not motivation. In other words, it takes more and more money to move people the same distance in terms of work and productivity. That is a far cry from people who have a passion for their work and intrinsically enjoy the challenge and relationships involved in pursuing it.

Prodding people with money is a bankrupt approach in developing a creative and productive culture. Establishing the expectation that "I should get paid for doing this, or else I will just do my job and go through the motions," is negative and eventually destructive. The culture that indicates "if you do that, you get this" stifles creative thinking because individuals get locked in a defined mind-set and standard way of accomplishing the work so they can get the reward.

In addition, the carrot-and-stick approach results in short-term thinking. "When institutions—families, schools, businesses, and athletic teams, for example—focus on the short term and opt for controlling people's behavior, they do considerable long-term damage."[16] A key result of this approach is that people forfeit some of their autonomy, lose control of their efforts, and limit the scope and depth of their thinking. Work becomes a "drudge" and begins to subtly promote negative behavior—cheating, taking shortcuts, and unethical behavior.

According to Pink, carrot-and-stick approaches leave dysfunctional residue. For example, in some districts across the country there have been examples of tampering with test results to produce the appearance of high performance.

Test score pressure has a dark side both ethically and educationally. The emphasis on achievement on standardized tests has given birth to educational "triage." The principle is the same as medical triage in the military: serve those who have the best odds to survive and let go of those who are too far gone. In essence, in education we focus on those students most who are only several questions away from reaching some semblance of proficiency, then don't place as much time on those students who are too far gone to reach the proficiency standard.

Those students who need only to answer a few more questions correctly to demonstrate proficiency can boost the school's overall achievement level.

Students who need to answer fifteen to twenty more questions correctly may not get there in the time before testing. So schools put their time and effort on helping students close to proficiency to get the desired metric.

Beer and Cannon of Harvard found in studying the issue at Hewlett-Packard that extrinsic incentives cause "employees to focus excessively on doing what they need to do to gain rewards, sometimes at the expense of doing other things that would help the organization."[17] Furthermore, another study concerning the performance of physicians found that "governments and private insurers throughout the world are likely wasting many billions of dollars on policies that assume that a financial incentive for patient health will improve quality of medical care."[18] They concluded that policy makers sometimes legislate large and expensive policies based on their beliefs without the requisite hard evidence, according to Stephen Soumerai, professor in the Department of Population Medicine at Harvard Medical School.

In other studies, researchers at the Harvard Business School found that there are psychological implications to the carrot-driven pay-for-performance systems. The psychological costs of pay-for-performance systems often dominate their benefits to firms. Professors Ian Larkin, Francesca Gino, and Lamar Pierce of Washington University conducted research and discussed an integrated theory of strategic compensation. Key concepts about the performance of physicians include:

> "Three psychological factors most prominently influence compensation strategy: social comparison processes, overconfidence, and loss aversion on the part of employees. Social comparison processes imply that employees care not only about their own pay but also about the pay of relevant others. If employees are overconfident about their abilities, which is often the case, they may become unmotivated or even engage in sabotage if they perceive unfair pay gaps between their and others' pay.
>
> Loss-averse employees are more motivated by potential failure to meet sometimes arbitrary levels of desired pay than they are by potential gains. This phenomenon implies that employees may work less hard than firms desire even if paid for performance. In response to these psychological factors, firms rely on flat salaries or "scale-based" systems where the pay-for-performance relationship is much less prominent than predicted by agency theory."[19]

Rewards may work for simple, narrowly focused tasks akin to paying your son to wash and wax the family car. There's a clear routine or procedure for any issue, with very little thinking involved. Teaching is not routine; problems and solutions are not always obvious and require creative and conceptual ability to work with the complexities of a classroom.

Quantitative engineers perceive the world in a mechanistic way. Because we worship at the altar of quantitative statistics, some have the idea that human beings will respond to economic incentives, hence the emphasis of reformers on so-called pay-for-performance, even though a small percentage of Americans are compensated in that manner. But the world does not operate with mechanistic regularity, which drives some command-and-control initiatives.

Schools do not respond to command and control because the problems are often difficult to diagnose and are complex. A single strategic maneuver will not resolve many of them satisfactorily or successfully. Professionals need the time to apply their knowledge and find solutions to the issues confronting them. A single stick of measurement flies in the face of the variables that teachers confront in their classrooms. We don't expect physicians, psychiatrists, lawyers, military officers, or others to apply a standard operating procedure to every circumstance they confront—the world is too complex and chaotic to respond to simple measures. Professionals use intuition and know when to deviate ethically from standard practice.

Intrinsic approaches, particularly around significant goals, motivate people to work harder and longer to achieve desired results. Professionals have the autonomy to make decisions on strategies and targets. If people commit to getting quality results on important goals, productivity rises, satisfaction increases, and turnover is reduced. Autonomy increases engagement.

Goals that people establish for themselves stimulate divergent thinking and insightful approaches. Goals strapped to teachers by others, particularly short-term ones, are not as enticing. Pink indicates, "goals imposed by others—sales targets, quarterly returns, standardized test scores, and so on—can sometimes have dangerous side effects. The addiction of being paid for every task or objective is destructive and causes people to feel manipulated."[20]

Therefore, organizations should pay people fairly, get the money carrot off the table, and then give individuals autonomy and support to complete their work. In schools, particularly, people seek a career as a teacher because of a sense of stewardship and wanting to make the lives of children better. There is built-in intrinsic impetus for teachers to work with their children, without regard to time, face difficult external issues that affect their children, and provide a nurturing environment for tackling high academic, creative, and character goals.

Pink has a very simple formula: autonomy + mastery + purpose = motivation.[21] The disconnect between what long-standing research says about motivation and the mythology that business and school organizations follow to get results from their employees has to be mended. Leaders' mind-set that organizations must demand conformity needs to be changed to one that applies the research-based fact that creativity demands autonomy to produce far more creative, innovative, and engaged schools.

Laying to rest the image of the "take no prisoners" leader who charges through schools, using sarcasm and fear and micro-managing may make celebrity icons, but does nothing for developing a culture that nourishes people's desire to reach important goals over the long term. Any change under a carrot-and-stick rubric is short-lived and fades after the so-called leaders leave. The Washington, D.C., schools are proof of that. In fact these leaders destroy potential, rather than develop it. Confusing movement and motivation is destructive.

SUMMARY

The charade of the "race to the top" mentality works against developing local school systems that would have the autonomy and ability to address the circumstances they face and find solutions. Sharing information between and among states and school systems would encourage others to review their practices and find better ways. Developing local and state "hothouses of innovation" to find and share solutions is more effective than "one size fits all" direction from Washington.

If the federal government has any role, it should be strictly limited to defining goals that inspire public school systems to achieve. People are motivated by goals and work to achieve them. Americans have traditionally responded to higher order goals, particularly without the rigidity of centralized control. Centralized procedural mandates stifle, stymie, and smother creativity and innovation.

Fragmentation, competition, and reactionary knee jerks are evident in today's organizations, including schools. We fragment problems into pieces yet problems are more systemic than simply symptoms or parts of a whole. We frequently take complex issues and turn them into symptoms and then treat the symptoms without addressing the real problem or concern.

Creative people need to work in conditions that are not exploitive or oppressive. They need to engage in a sense of cooperative teamwork and not alienation. They must know clearly what is expected in terms of performance so that they can use their autonomy to reach those expectations. Our current organizational structure that fragments knowledge and creates overspecialization of roles works against synthesizing diverse information and finding breakthroughs that improve results.

NOTES

1. Linda Darling-Hammond and Edward Haertel, "A Better Way to Grade Teachers," *Los Angeles Times*, November 5, 2012.

2. Richard Rothstein, *How to Fix Our Schools* (Washington, DC: Economic Policy Institute, October 14, 2010), www.epi.org/publication/ib286/

3. Mihaly Csikszentmihalyi, *Creativity* (New York: HarperCollins Publishers, 1996), 28.

4. Ken Robinson, *Out of Our Minds: Learning to Be Creative* (New York: Wiley, 2011, 197).

5. Ken Robinson and Lou Aronica, *The Element* (New York: Viking, 2009), 70.

6. Teresa Amabile and Mukti Khaire, "Creativity and the Role of the Leader," *Harvard Business Review*, October 2008.

7. Margaret Wheatley, *Leadership and the New Science* (San Francisco, CA: Berrett-Koehler Publishers, 1992), 88.

8. Wheatley, *Leadership and the New Science*, 104.

9. Robinson and Aronica, *The Element*, 220.

10. Amabile and Khaire, "Creativity and the Role of the Leader."

11. Frederick Herzberg, "One More Time: How Do You Motivate Employees?" *Harvard Business Review*, January 2003.

12. Frederick W. Taylor, *Principles of Scientific Management* (New York: Harper & Brothers, 1911), 229.

13. J. W. Rinehart, *The Tyranny of Work*, Canadian Social Problems Series, Academic Press Canada, 1975, 44.

14. Daniel Pink, *Drive: The Surprising Truth about What Motivates Us* (New York: Riverhead Books, 2009).

15. Herzberg, ibid. 2003.

16. Pink, *Drive*, 37.

17. Michael Beer and Mark D. Cannon, "The Promise and Peril in Implementing Pay for Performance," *Human Resource Development* 43, no. 1 (Spring 2004): 82–89.

18. B. Serumaga, D. Ross-Degnan, A. J. Avery, R. A. Elliot, S. R. Majumdar, F. Zhang, and S. B. Soumerai, "Effect of Pay for Performance on the Management Outcomes of Hypertension in the United Kingdom: Interrupted Times Series Study," *British Medical Journal* 342 (2011): 322.

19. Ian Larken, L. Pierce, and Francis Gino, "The Psychological Costs of Pay for Performance: Implications for the Strategic Compensation of Employees," *Strategic Management Journal* 33, no. 10 (October 2012): 1194–1214.

20. Pink, *Drive*, 48.

21. "Dan Pink: The Puzzle of Motivation," TED Talks, August 25, 2009, www.ted.com/talks/dan_pink_on_motivation.html

Chapter Eight

Culture Matters

Over the past thirty years, as we have shown, there has been a significant shift in educational policy, where the impetus for policy and reform moved from local and state government to the federal level. This is contrary to an important governing concept in the United States: government decision making should be close to the people.

Parents, local school boards, and citizens closest to the welfare and education of children should make those decisions. We have moved quite a distance from this concept as federal carrot-and-stick fiscal policies push education at the local level to adopt federal policies affecting standards, curriculum, assessment, and accountability. This impetus for greater regulation, mandates, and prescribed programs has a significant effect on school cultures, climate, working conditions, and the ability of teachers and principals to respond creatively to the needs of students.

Reformers rail against union-negotiated master contract clauses and their rule-driven impact on school operations. The reformers' approach to transforming education, however, takes the same route—mandates and regulations that create top-down, rigid, and rule-driven organizational cultures. Teacher evaluation based on short-term test scores, for example, has resulted in teachers teaching to tests and discarding or reducing emphasis on content, concepts, or analytical and critical thinking that do not easily succumb to standardized test regimens.

Rule-driven and highly controlled organizations based on bureaucratic rules and red tape do not result in adaptive and innovative organizations. Frederick Taylor's scientific management is alive and well in school reform initiatives. As columnist Eugene Robinson of the *Washington Post* states, "School reform cannot be something that ostensibly smart, ostentatiously tough 'superstar' superintendents do to a school system and the people who depend on it. Reform has to be something that is done *with* a community of teachers, students and parents—with honesty and, yes, a bit of old-fashioned humility."[1]

All of this raises the issue of what do we want our school organizations to be. Should they be rule-driven, machinelike bureaucracies, or should they be creative and collaborative organizations? There are big differences between these two approaches, their goals and climate, as well as how people are perceived and treated, all of which affect their performance and success.

ORGANIZATIONAL CULTURE

Organizational cultures matter. They are not platitudinous concepts that are the domain of graduate courses or corporate marketing. Corporate culture determines how people are treated, how talent is perceived, and how work gets completed.

Corporate culture, in service or private-sector organizations, determines the "rules of the game" for structure, decision making, and how work gets done. Culture rests on defined values and beliefs and translates into desired behavior in pursuing the mission of the organization. In other words, corporate culture defines the guiding ideas of the organization, and the principles and ideas that matter. Organizational culture is translated through beliefs and assumptions about people, motivation, creativity, and procedural structures. They shape "organizational practices, guide how people do things, and, in turn, determine what skills and capabilities people develop based on those organizational practices."[2]

Organizational cultures are unique in that they consist of "ideas and beliefs that constitute what some philosophers call *Weltanschauung*, or worldview. Different worldviews give rise to different ways of evaluating experience and to different forms of behavior."[3] Robinson indicates that culture gets translated into codes of conduct that define what is acceptable and unacceptable, including such things as attitude, dress, language, actions, and more, enforced through the formal and/or informal organization and leadership.

Culture impacts the attitude and drive of people working within the organization. Some may find the culture stimulating and others may find it suppressing. If it is perceived as suppressive, individuals will not meet their potential and will find that where they work is a "bad fit" for them. Organizational culture is a critical factor in motivation. If employees believe in the cultural values and principles of the organization, they will work hard to be true to them.

Today, we marvel at organizations like Apple and Google for their creative products, technical breakthroughs, and innovation. Conversely, we are repulsed by the Department of Motor Vehicles or insurance companies with their standard operating procedures, rigid attitude and lack of discretion in addressing our individual needs. The cultural differences are apparent to you and the people working in them. Cultures differ and that difference has an impact on commitment, motivation, and attitude within the organization.

Basically, four organizational cultures are apparent, each with different perspectives and values.[4] All may be valid, depending on the nature of the work and goals of the organization. A short description of the characteristics is defined below.

Controlled organizational cultures are concerned primarily with order and being tightly aligned with measurable goals and objectives, resulting in a hierarchy of reporting procedures with power and authority residing at the top of the organizational ladder. Getting the numbers and meeting measurable targets are a priority, usually in quarterly or annual performance evaluations. In this culture consistency and regimentation are virtues. These organizations are very bureaucratic with designated rules, procedures, and processes, resulting in red tape and paperwork in order to monitor their progress. Employees do not have much discretion in decision making. Decisions must be reviewed and approved by "management," with individual creativity taking a backseat to maintaining order. The status quo lives! Success means the dependable delivery of outcomes and standardized results.

Some organizational cultures are highly *competitive*—both internally and externally. Personal and team achievement is primary, and individual accomplishment is valued more than teamwork. Consequently, personal knowledge, skill, and aggressive attitudes are prized. Leaders have a "take no prisoners" attitude and are demanding and hard driving. Winning and beating the competition on specific measurable goals is central. Think standardized test scores. The downside to this culture is that individuals do not share insights and ideas, which works against teamwork, and sometimes they cut ethical corners leading to cheating and deceptive practices. Books can be cooked and false data and comparisons are used to demonstrate success and hide shortfalls or failures.

Collaborative cultures take a different view. The primary drivers are teamwork and consensus. Commitment to a common purpose and shared decision making are a priority. Trustworthiness and teamwork are valued above aggressiveness and even creativity. Relationships matter, both internally and externally with employees and clients. Cohesion, loyalty, and morale are important. In these collaborative cultures, decision making is slower because discussion of options and alternatives and the evaluation of each take time. Getting consensus is not always easy or fast. Thoughtfulness, based on teamwork, is highly valued.

Finally, some organizations reject highly competitive, controlled or collaborative cultures and place their emphasis on *creativity and individual self-expression*. Keeping imaginative and brilliant people is highly valued. These organizations celebrate innovative individuals and teams that can self-organize and develop new approaches and improved outcomes. Research and development are important drivers. Innovation and risk taking are prized, with a strong commitment to experimentation. Employees have flexibility and discretion, along with the ability to adapt to changing times and conditions. Being a recognized leader in the field is an organizational goal. These organizations are dynamic, not bureaucratic.

A CULTURE OF CREATIVITY

A major issue is whether the culture of schools suppresses or stimulates talent and commitment. While politicians and the business sector bash teachers, the same sources carp about the need for highly talented and imaginative people in the profession. They fail to see, however, that hierarchical control and power-driven cultures work against attracting talented people. In fact, they are a detractor to anyone who wants professional autonomy and creative ability to work with children to create a learning environment that is developmentally appropriate and exciting.

Fortune magazine, in their annual survey of best companies to work for, highlights the attributes the companies possess.[5] Certainly good workplaces have communication that involves employees in developing objectives and working to fulfill the organization's mission. Employees receive regular and candid updates about where the organization is headed and are included in helping the organization achieve their goals. Transparency exists, meaning individuals do not hide information, but share it and build trust. Employees are not ordered what to do, but share in the opportunity to establish targets and set strategies.

Individuals have the ability to innovate and have the freedom to experiment and develop fresh ideas. They are invited to contribute ideas, to comment on them, and to engage in collaborative efforts to find solutions to the problems they face. They have time to think, and a real dialogue between and among the individuals exists.

Creativity does not happen in isolation. Robinson states, "Creativity is about making connections and more often than not . . . is driven by collaboration as much as, if not more than, solo efforts."[6] He indicates, "Cultures that enforce strict boundaries between 'specialisms' can inhibit potentially valuable forms of innovation."

Working in a collaborative team is another factor in people committing to their jobs. Individuals are encouraged to continue their attempts to do better and find solutions to difficult problems and issues. Fear of reprisal or a "gotcha" environment destroys participation, trust, and innovation.

CREATIVE ENVIRONMENTS IN EDUCATION

Google's culture is innovative and change-prone with competent and committed employees who are passionate about innovating.[7] Leadership has a high degree of trust and sees their role as empowering, coaching, and removing obstacles from their employees. It is a nonbureaucratic organization. Employees are dedicated to continuous learning. Leaders believe that new and good ideas can come from anyone and anywhere in the organization, and not simply from top management.

Contemporary reform proposals create organizational cultures that are a far cry from the likes of innovative organizations. Professional autonomy of teachers is not particularly valued, as programs and instruction are standardized. Uniformity of methods and processes based on simplistic test outcomes is characteristic of many reform movements.

Unfortunately, many reformers do not see teachers as professionals or teaching as a particularly creative profession by virtue of the standardization and "group think" advocated and managed in schools. However, teaching is a creative profession according to Robinson. He states, "There are many good teachers whose creative instincts are curbed by standardized education and whose effectiveness is diminished as a result. A creative culture in schools depends on re-energizing the creative ability of teachers."[8]

According to W. Edwards Deming, "A manager of people needs to understand that all people are different. This is not ranking people. He needs to understand that the performance of anyone is governed largely by the system that he works in, the responsibility of management."[9]

In a *New Yorker* article David Denby profiles Diane Ravitch about the reform movement in education.[10] Ravitch states that the movement is "united by the assumption that, despite the existence of some great and many good schools, and despite the vast expenditures, American public education is in bad shape." She goes on to indicate that reformers insist on test-based accountability and choice, plus pay based on merit and bonuses, the elimination of tenure, and the revision of contracts complete with no due process clauses. Cultures based on these principles do not inspire innovation or talent.

In the Denby interview, Ravitch states that testing is valuable because it reveals gaps. However, "if you want people to be creative and entrepreneurial, forget test scores. It's character that makes success." She cautions that "students can be coaxed to guess the right answer, but learning this skill does not equate to acquiring facility in complex reasoning and analysis. It is possible to have higher test scores and worse education. The scores tell us nothing about how students think, how deeply they understand history or science or literature or philosophy or how prepared they are to cast their votes carefully or be wise jurors."[11]

Many individuals, according to Robinson, see education simply as preparation for employment. "The assumption that there is a direct linear relationship between general education and subsequent employment puts schools under pressure to prioritize those subjects that seem relevant to the economy."[12] The curriculum becomes narrowed to a hierarchy of disciplines with math, languages, and science at the top. He indicates that since NCLB districts have "eliminated or seriously reduced their arts programs" where creativity and innovative thought are valued.[13]

Ravitch and Robinson are not alone. Senge in his article *Creating Schools of the Future: Education for a Sustainable Future,* states that schools of the future should focus on more than test scores. "While mainstream school systems are obsessed with standardized test scores and intense individual competition, education innovators are focused on higher-order skills like systems thinking and creativity in conjunction with basic skills in mathematics and language; personal maturation together with technical knowledge; and learning how to learn together in service of addressing problems that are real."[14]

If we expect schools to become creative "learning organizations," then the old models will not get you there. In Senge's book *Schools That Learn*, he cites W. Edwards Deming as stating that the prevailing system of management has "destroyed our people because of its impacts on intrinsic motivation, curiosity, risk taking and innovation, and personal responsibility."[15]

THE REALITY OF POVERTY AND EDUCATION

Scapegoating teachers in reform movements destroys the motivation and restricts professional educators. In pushing for a system of performance and accountability, reformers like Joel Klein, former chancellor of the New York City Department of Education, stated, "I reject categorically the principle that poverty is an insurmountable impediment, because I see that we have surmounted it time and again."[16]

Rothstein indicates that "it's when poverty combined with chaos at home, adult illiteracy, neglect, unaddressed health issues, constant dislocation, and a neighborhood pervaded by addiction and crime that most children in these environments become, in sociologist William Julius Wilson's phrase, 'truly disadvantaged.' It's these children whose academic performance we must help to improve and who are the target of most self-described school reformers."[17]

When Klein, Michelle Rhee, and Secretary Duncan state that teachers alone determine whether children succeed in school and deride home environment as merely an obstacle, they are simply wrong. Rothstein goes on to say that "even the best teachers face impossible tasks when confronted with classrooms filled with truly disadvantaged students who are not in tracked special-progress classes and don't arrive each morning from families as academically supportive as mine. Instead they may come from segregated communities were concentrated and entrenched poverty, unemployment, and social alienation over many generations have been ravaging."[18]

Rothstein indicates that the school reform policies have resulted in needless test obsessions for millions of schoolchildren with the idea that test score–based accountability will solve children's learning needs, even from the homes he describes above. Teachers are not miracle workers. And taking a position that teachers are almost solely responsible has produced "turmoil" and little or no meaningful improvement in schools for highly disadvantaged children.

Education has always been perceived to be the door to greater opportunity, success, and happiness for all people, especially those in poverty. Education and opportunity are almost synonymous.

Lane Kenworthy, writes that "inequality of opportunity has increased in recent decades. . . . Available compilations of test scores, years of schooling completed, occupations, and incomes of parents and their children strongly suggest that the opportunity gap, which was narrowing until the 1970s, is now widening."[19]

Kenworthy is in community with Rothstein concerning low-income families and their condition outside of school. He states that

> the share of poorer children growing up with both biological parents has fallen sharply, whereas there has been less change among the wealthy. About 88% of children from high-income homes grew up with married parents. That is down from 96% four decades ago. Meanwhile, only 41% of poor children grow up in homes with married parents, down 77% from four decades ago. That has hurt our children's chance of success, since those who live with both of their parents are more likely, even accounting for income, to fare better in school, stay out of trouble with the law, maintain lasting relationships, and earn higher incomes as adults.[20]

In addition, Kenworthy indicates that low-income parents do not have the resources to spend on goods and services that help enrich children's lives, such as music lessons, travel, and summer camps. These parents tend to read less to their children and provide less help with schoolwork. They are also not as likely to set and enforce clear rules and routines for their children, and include the lack of encouragement for the children to aspire to high achievement in school and work.

Research by the economist James Heckman and others, cited by Kenworthy, indicates that much of the gap in cognitive and noncognitive skills between children from poor homes and those from affluent homes is already present by the time they enter kindergarten. This has resulted in large differences between children of high-income families and those from low-income families on test scores. "Among children born in 1970, those from high-income homes scored, on average, about three-quarters of the standard deviation higher on math and reading tests than those from low-income homes. Among children born in 2000, the gap has grown to one and a quarter standard deviations. That is much larger than the gap between white and black children."[21]

Placing the responsibility for achievement gaps and the performance of low-income children squarely on the shoulders of teachers basically is a straw dog. Teachers have children in their classrooms for approximately six to seven hours. How can anyone think that they can take highly disadvantaged children who live within the context described by both Rothstein and Kenworthy and be solely responsible for student achievement on tests? This is ludicrous. Meanwhile those reformers who talk tough, including Klein, Rhee, and Duncan, neglect some of the real causes of student achievement, not only in test scores, but also in getting a high-quality, broad-based education that involves analytical thinking, ethics, principles, concepts, culture, and wisdom.

SUMMARY

Public education in America has been on a slippery slope of change through mandated and coercive funding and sanction. The key challenge is to create and sustain public schools that truly educate children coming from all social economic and ethnic backgrounds, establishing school cultures and climates that support both children and attract high-quality, talented, and inspired educators. To do so requires developing school organizations that are adaptable and innovative today and in the future, and providing organizations not based on command-and-control but on a collaborative and creative culture. Finally, it involves instituting an accountability system that makes sense and is based on the long-term, rather than short-term, politically inspired approaches.

NOTES

1. Eugene Robinson, "The Racket with Standardized Test Scores," *Washington Post*, April 1, 2013.
2. Peter Senge, *The Fifth Discipline* (New York: Currency, 2006), 285.
3. Ken Robinson, *Out of Our Minds: Learning to Be Creative* (New York: Wiley, 2011), 205–6.
4. Bruce M. Tharp, "Four Organizational Culture Types," www.haworth.com/docs/default-source/white-papers/four-organizational-culture--types_6-pdf-28545.pdf
5. "100 Best Companies to Work For," *Fortune*, February 6, 2012.
6. Robinson, *Out of Our Minds*, 211–12.
7. Annika Steiber, *Organizational Innovation: A Conceptualization of How They Are Created, Diffused, and Sustained* (Gothenberg, Sweden: Chalmers University of Technology, 2012).
8. Robinson, *Out of Our Minds*, 267.
9. W. Edwards Deming, *The New Economics for Industry, Government, Education,* 2nd edition (Cambridge, MA: MIT Press, 1993).
10. Denby, David. "Public Defender: Diane Ravitch Takes on a Movement." *New Yorker*, November 19, 2012, www.newyorker.com/reporting/2012/11/19/121119fa_fact_denby
11. Denby, "Public Defender: Ravitch Takes on a Movement," *New Yorker*, November 19, 2012.
12. Robinson, *Out of Our Minds*, 59.
13. Robinson, *Out of Our Minds*, 62.
14. Peter Senge, "Creating Schools of the Future: Education for a Sustainable Future," *The Solutions Journal*, June 2012.
15. Peter Senge, *Schools That Learn* (New York: Currency, 2000), 46.
16. "High Hopes: Chancellor of New York City Public Schools," *PBS Newshour*, September 30, 2002. www.pbs.org/newshour/bb/education/july-dec02/nyc_9-30.html
17. Richard Rothstein, "Slight of Hand," *American Prospect*, November/December 2012, 38.
18. Rothstein, "Slight of Hand," 38.
19. Kenworthy, Lane, "Why It's Hard to Make It in America," *Foreign Affairs* 91, no.6 (November–December 2012): 99.
20. Kenworthy, "Why It's Hard to Make It in America," 100.
21. Kenworthy, "Why It's Hard to Make It in America," 101–2.

Chapter Nine

So What Does This All Mean?

We must break out of our straitjacket and give schools more flexibility in finding creative and innovative ways to address the needs of students, changing times, and professional expectations—not shackle them through regulatory mandates, closed thinking, and defective accountability processes.

Over the last thirty years the system has hamstrung educators and parents in creating schools responsive to children's needs today and in the future. Short-term fixes, the narrowing of the curriculum, regulations and mandates coming from Washington and state capitals, and short-sighted educators who succumb to fiscally coercive approaches must stop. It is not going to be easy.

Those who see profit and markets as the answer have weakened public support for schools. In addition, misinterpretations and the selective interpretation and use of research for particular purposes have degraded the dialogue. We focus on achievement gaps, not preparation gaps that address the root cause of lagging achievement. And we look to short-term test results, not long-term student care and progress.

In all of this, there are no easy answers. But public education has been a stalwart institution and the foundation for our democracy. Public education, like all institutions and fields—medicine, law, politics, business, and Wall Street—is not without its failings. Subverting it, however, will only weaken our democracy and diminish what an education ought to be for our children.

Public education has to be changed, not destroyed. To do so requires a long view, not quick fixes. A primary issue is defining the real problems in educating children with diverse needs. The recommendations we are making are, in some cases, fundamental and involve rethinking what schools ought to be by looking to see what has worked in the past, and what children need for the future. In other cases, recommendations require changes in perspective and thinking that some may think are improbable and too difficult because of politics and influence. We think these recommendations are based on the common good, and not on the self-interests of ideologues or private sector interests. Some initiatives are easier to attain than others, and some may take a longer time to realize because of the political processes that must be tackled to achieve them.

We stand on several foundations for action when it comes to improving education for all children and fostering and growing public education's continued impact. They are fundamental to the development and success of local school districts' and educators' creative problem solving and innovative programming. The following six foundations guide the recommendations found in the final chapter of the book. These foundations represent a summary of the issues, concerns, theories, and realities we've discussed throughout the prior chapters.

FOUNDATION ONE—DEFINE AN EDUCATED PERSON

The first foundation is a matter of definition. In improving schools, the first step is to define what an educated person is. This is the most basic of all questions. Without defining what an educated person is, we cannot determine what changes or reforms our public schools must confront. The current reforms assume that testing, primarily in math, writing, and reading, will achieve educational excellence. But in actuality, literacy and mathematical skills are third world educational goals. An education is much more than what is tested in these areas.

We can't settle for merely testing literacy or mathematics. There are aspects to being educated that cannot be assessed in the immediate time frame but are only revealed in a person's decisions in life. We used to talk of the importance of wisdom and learning high-minded principles with an eye on the common good. Wisdom concerns how people use their knowledge and apply it to the complexities of contemporary life. All children deserve an education that is greater than simply the acquisition of skills. There are plenty of examples of skilled people who make decisions that corrupt personal or social values.

According to Robert Sternberg, professor and director of the Center for the Psychology of Abilities, Competence, and Expertise (PACE), "We are teaching students to be intelligent and knowledgeable, but not how to use their intelligence and knowledge. Schools need to teach for wisdom, not just factual recall and superficial levels of analysis."[1]

The current penchant for standardized testing has restricted the curriculum, and eliminated content and concepts that are necessary for a life filled with unimaginable change and innovation. One only has to look at the changes that took place from the earliest twentieth century to the turn of the twenty-first century to see that education for today's jobs in today's society will not be sufficient for a happy and successful life in a changing future.

Businesses, according to deGues, have a much shorter life span than human beings do. "The average life expectancy of a multinational corporation—Fortune 500 or its equivalent—is between 40 and 50 years. . . . Human beings have learned to survive, on average, for 75 years or more, but there are very few companies that are that old and flourishing.[2]

Thus, those who think the goal of education is to train people for jobs in today's economy are on a fool's errand. Many of the present jobs will not exist, and new ones about which we have no conception, will erupt as technology, innovation, and transformations in the political and international context come about.

The purpose of education is not only to provide workers for corporations or businesses, nor is it just to understand math, science, technology, and engineering. While there is virtue to competence in these areas, they are not sufficient for an individual to address all of the roles that adults must play in our society. People are not just workers; they are citizens, parents, service workers, family members, entrepreneurs, creators, neighbors, artists, mentors, public officials, change agents, police officers, philosophers, and a host of other roles.

The most recent national effort to have a "common core" standard for education across the country specifies what skills and knowledge students need to be prepared for postsecondary education and the workforce. These new standards focus on English/Language Arts and Mathematics, with literacy in History/Social Studies, Science, and technical subjects. The "common core" is supposed to take the place of existing state standards.

A major concern about the new standards is the further narrowing of the curriculum. Not reflected in them are art, music, dance, ethics, and philosophy. We live and work in a culture and the rudiments of culture are important to quality of life. The focus on career readiness presupposes we know what skills will be necessary twenty years down the line when a kindergartener enters the workforce after college. A narrowed curriculum results in narrow schooling around test-friendly content.

These standards were released in 2010, and some critics argue that the standards were not field-tested, educator's input was limited, and there is no data to indicate they will raise achievement in those areas or restrict achievement. Other criticism concerns the influence of private and corporate interests like the Gates Foundation and Pearson Corporation. The Gates Foundation contributed funds for the development of the standards and is underwriting

Pearson's program to develop online courses and other resources related to them.

The fear is that the "common core" will result in a *mandated* national testing program and eliminate local control even further. Few classroom teachers were involved in their development. Further, the cost of implementation of the standards is projected to be extremely costly to states and local districts.

This gets back to the need to define what an educated person is. It is certainly more than the accumulation of facts. Critical, divergent, and complex thinking are important in any era and leads to creativity and innovation. Literature, music, and all the fine arts are essential for a comprehensive education. Citizens should debate the issue of who controls public education, not corporations or other special interest groups.

FOUNDATION TWO: THERE IS A DIFFERENCE BETWEEN EDUCATION AND SCHOOLING

There is a difference between being well educated and well schooled. The great philosophical questions of life—truth, beauty, justice, liberty, equality, and goodness—cannot be assessed through a computer-scored test. Searching for the answers to these issues is at the very core of our society and the essence of becoming well educated.

These great ideas should be studied in school and understood by our children if they are to live a life of depth, understanding, and principle. This requires a broad education in the academics, fine arts, and culture. An education is more than simply getting a job or meeting a career goal. It is more than training. Chasing the brass ring without a strong foundation in principle can be corrupting.

All of our children, rich and poor, should be educated so they can contribute to the common good, be responsible and active citizens, and adapt to changing times. Being able to think critically, to pose questions as well as seek answers, and to understand and develop an ethical and moral framework are a part of being well educated. Educated people have strong academic skills, but they also have the values and principles that form the foundation for their life's decisions and a successful society. These include the acquisition of knowledge, but also the development of intellectual skills, as well as a deep understanding of ideas and values and "exercising critical judgment."[3]

Well-educated people revere knowledge and apply values and principles to guide them as they seek a meaningful life of purpose. They try to make "wise" decisions premised on strong ethical and moral ideals, coupled with a broad academic and cultural understanding.

Education is a lifelong process of continuous learning and examination. Being well educated means having a sense of stewardship and a concern for the common good, not simply tending to self-interest and ego needs.

Parents frequently say they want their children to attend a "good" school. As we said earlier, a good school is not one between excellent and poor. For children to grow, develop and prosper they need a place of "goodness"; a sanctuary for learning filled with respect for individuals, reverence for principles and ideas, encouragement of talent and dreams, and preparation for a life well lived.

If we ask ourselves the fundamental difference between being well schooled or well educated, maybe we can turn our schools into sanctuaries for our children to become not only highly literate but also *wise* and *cultured* so they can fulfill themselves and pursue their happiness with a sense of stewardship.

Creativity, imagination, joy, ingenuity, wonder, and idealism must not be wrung from our schools. These intangibles are the foundation of the success of our country and are the basis for a well-educated and civil society. It is well documented that a test-oriented and competitive school culture reduces the scope of the educational program and ignores the fact that some facets of a child's education and development cannot be easily quantified. Issues of values, ethics, and character are beyond the bounds of tests, as are complex concepts, analytical and critical thinking, and creativity and imagination.

Parents, politicians, and other "influentials" must define what they mean by an educated person, who will be able to live a life of meaning and purpose, as well as contribute their talents, perspectives, and skills to our nation's society, economy, and families.

FOUNDATION THREE: WIDEN THE CORRIDOR OF DECISION MAKING

A third foundation is the necessity to widen the discretionary corridor of decision making to allow for inventive, imaginative, inspired and resourceful decision making at the local school and community level. To do so requires reducing the influence of centralized control specifically from the federal government. In this case, the foundation of less centralized government is better for creative and innovative schools. Limiting the role of the U.S. Department of Education is pivotal.

The federal department of education as a cabinet position did not exist prior to 1979. The cabinet status of this department was debated fiercely, particularly around whether or not the federal government had or should have control over education in the United States. The way the federal government has pursued educational interests in both Democratic and Republican administrations has been through the lure of money. In order to get financing under No Child Left Behind (NCLB), states and local governments had to adopt certain programs and procedures in order to adhere to mandates and regulations.

Remember, the federal government has no constitutional authority concerning education. There are fifty states, each with a department of education, the redundancy is unnecessary as well as costing the states money to implement the federal program mandates.

Proponents of maintaining the department basically argue that the federal government could never be reorganized, that rescinding legislation is next to impossible, particularly as it applies to bureaucratic departments. As we indicated earlier, the record of the federal impact on achievement is not positive. Under the Obama administration, carrots and sticks are used for states to get federal funding to support schools, provided they follow a regimen and regulations under the "Race to the Top" initiative. Thus, the role of the federal government expanded, regulations have increased, paperwork swelled, and costs exploded.

Initiatives like test-based accountability and teacher evaluation and the contraction of the curricular program have taken place. State resources also had to be allocated, stymieing many local and state initiatives. The centralization of education in Washington politicizes it in central legislative and executive bodies, making it easier for private sector and other political interests to lobby for their self-interest in one venue, rather than each state capitol.

Reducing the role of the federal department in education would require government reorganization. No easy task. The size of the federal government and its expansion of departments and regulatory agencies has grown steadily over the last fifty years. This recommendation is made with the understanding that this change would be hotly debated and difficult to implement.

The concept of "localness" is connected to reducing or eliminating the role of the federal Department of Education. The further from the local and state government initiatives and regulations are, the less people have ownership in and understand them. That is why the concept of broad principles at the state level can best be met by individuals closest to the issues entering into a dialogue[4] and debate about the best way to live those values in their school district and schools.

Ownership is a key factor. Just implementing programs filled with red tape at the local level to get some semblance of funding has unintended consequences. A major unintended consequence, for example, is that pressure to make short-term results has reduced the total educational experience for children.

The federal government is one of the major reasons why the corridor of decision making, discretion, creativity, and innovation is narrowing on individual school districts across the country. Since the federal government increased control, there's little evidence to prove that school improvement has taken place. In fact the case could be made otherwise.

FOUNDATION FOUR: TEACHERS ARE THE SOLUTION, NOT THE PROBLEM

A major issue in school reform is our perception of the role of teachers. Some people view them as laborers, yet they perceive themselves as professionals. In fact, most people do. This raises a major issue. Professionals have different needs than laborers and technicians because the expectations and demands on them are stronger and more diverse.

Teachers are not bureaucrats either. However, many of the reforms view them in that fashion. Professionals and bureaucrats function differently at work. The work of bureaucrats is programmed by the system, and they are subordinate to it. Hierarchical bureaucracies are dysfunctional for professionals because they operate in rule-driven ways and emphasize standardized behavior. Professional work involves autonomy, challenge, variety, and meaning. Joseph H. Raelin outlines the precepts under which professionals work:

- Expertise: specialized training in abstract knowledge
- Autonomy: the ability to choose the examination of and the means to solve problems
- Commitment: primary interest in pursuing the practice of the profession
- Identification: identify with the profession or fellow professionals to form associations or external referents
- Ethics: rendering service without regard for oneself and in the best interests of the client
- Standards: committing oneself to policing their personal conduct and that of fellow professionals.[5]

Goens and Clover state, "The contrast between professional and bureaucratic principles leads to role conflict: the incongruence between the needs of individuals driven by professional standards, and the organizational expectations of bureaucracies. Bureaucratic principles include job specialization, standardization, and centralization of authority. Professionals have a different perspective, however. They stress the uniqueness of clients' needs, achievement, research, change, and skill based on knowledge. Authority is based on competence, not position, and loyalty is to professional standards and clients."[6]

Table 9.1 identifies the contrast between bureaucratic and professional principles below:[7]

Teachers centered on professional principles are supposed to defend the welfare of students and implement teaching strategies and methods to help them learn. In some schools, however, teachers are expected to use a method that is prescribed and designated by the organization and follow school procedures and regulations. This view of professional teaching as defined by student needs and appropriate practice has often clashed with hierarchical managers who see rules as universals to be implemented without question.

Schools that operate mechanistically keep professionals subordinate to administrative controls and limit their discretion and autonomy. In professional organic organizations, professionals should have the responsibility for defining and implementing goals, establishing performance standards, and ensuring that the standards are maintained. The clash of different expectations in these two organizations creates conflict. The question is: which organizational structure is going to produce the greatest positive results for individual students through school?

As Goens and Clover assert, ethics must be the cornerstone of any professional service or treatment in order to provide security to clients: in this case, children.[8] In bureaucracies, people often pass the buck, indicating that it was not "their job," and finger pointing becomes endemic. Ethically, teachers have responsibilities for their own actions and for the actions they initiate and undertake under the direction of others. They also implicitly have responsibility for their actions if they are part of a group and therefore must defend against "group-think" or going along with the crowd when it is not in the best interest of students.

Table 9.1. Bureaucratic versus Professional Organizations

	Bureaucratic	Professional
Standardization	• Stress uniformity of client problems • Rules as universals • Stress record-keeping	• Stress uniqueness of client problems • Rules as alternatives • Stress research and change
Specialization	• Efficiency of techniques: task orientation • Skill based on practice	• Achievement of goals: client orientation • Skill based on knowledge
Authority	• Decisions based on application of rules • Loyalty to organization • Authority from position	• Decisions based on unique problems • Loyalty to client • Authority from competence

It is imperative then that in evaluating teachers that ethical precepts should be an integral part of the process. In that regard, they should have to confront the same accountability as other professionals, such as lawyers, physicians, or psychologists in terms of standards of care. Just evaluating them based on a principal's observation of certain techniques or practices, or student performance on short-term tests may not be appropriate or effective in increasing teacher performance. Students are not all the same, particularly if they suffer from a preparation gap because of home conditions or other factors.

Teachers also need to keep abreast of new research, as well as have time to think, refresh, and reflect. Professional development should move beyond fundamental training to larger questions of conceptual understanding and dialogue. Training, while necessary, should not be reduced to simple process experience or "painting by numbers," as is often the case. Understanding the values and principles of a school organization is fundamental. Values guide practice.

As we indicated earlier, a positive culture for growth and to encourage innovation is essential for attracting talented people and for educating children in developmentally appropriate ways. Successful organizations of all stripes are strong on values and creativity. Those that are rigid and don't adapt fail.

Senge's work on learning organizations is an essential part of creating high-performing, committed, and meaningful organizations. In examining the work of William O'Brien, who was a central focus of his book, *The Fifth Discipline*,[9] he found that O'Brien reorganized a floundering organization into a highly successful one through values and principles. O'Brien stated, "We came back to the values and vision in every major meeting. And we walked the talk. . . . We always came back to 'what is our vision? What are values? How does our purpose tell us what to do?'"[10] To define and understand the values that undergird a creative and productive culture takes time, conversation, and dialogue.

Thinking about these issues requires a very different set of questions to guide a theory of action. These might include questions such as:

- What do we need to do to unfreeze the school system, that is, free principals and teachers from unnecessary regulation and top-down governance structures and requirements?
- How can we maximize distributive leadership in districts and schools?
- How can we define outcomes differently beyond the traditional culture of student achievement testing?
- What do we need to do to unleash teacher creativity and promote experimentation without teachers fearing that their students' "failure" to achieve

standards will bring retribution in the form of dire consequences for employment decisions and reputations?

School leaders also need continued education on the development and analysis of *qualitative* as well as quantitative information. First, turning data into information and understanding the dangers of data manipulation and interpretation are critical. The essential failure to understand assessment literacy has led to many of the problems we face today with failed policy. In addition, they require training in qualitative research and analysis because many of the competencies and characteristics of educated people are not quantitative in nature.

Professional development should assist educators with defining a theory of action based on the values of the organization.[11] In addition, a "standard of care" should be defined and discussed, along with the usual standards that must be met in defining appropriate practice and innovation. This standard of care should be tied to the values of the school, but also to the ethics and principles of professional teacher and educator associations.

FOUNDATION FIVE: SCHOOLS ARE DYNAMIC ORGANIZATIONS

A fourth foundation is that schools do not exist in cocoons immune to the external environment. Neither do children. Powerful forces are at play in children's lives that affect their learning, focus, motivation, and self-concept. The data on the impact of poverty, family, and neighborhood conditions are clear on this issue.

We seem to understand that adults who are going through divorce, who are impoverished and underfed, who live in communities that are drug infested and unsafe, who confront health issues and other problems are not as productive at work or in other facets of their lives. But when it comes to children, there is the delusion that a teacher with a class with twenty-five to thirty youngsters can erase the hunger, dysfunctionality of families, drugs, alcohol, or the abuse- and violence-infested context in which they live. Teachers are not superhuman, nor do they have the resources at their disposal to heal families, feed, clothe, and house children. And given all of the issues they deal with, teachers do not have the ability to restructure or revise the early childhood upbringing of these children to include reading readiness, vocabulary development, and an appreciation for education.

Rothstein states "I suggested that he [Joel Klein, former chancellor of the New York City Department of Education] might win more lasting achievement gains by establishing school clinics to ensure that all children have good healthcare and by directing resources to early-childhood literacy programs and afterschool enrichment."[12]

Our view holds that the federal and state governments should fully support and implement the following programs to address these confounding issues.

- Preschool education programs in areas of poverty
- Health care and nutritional support for children of parents in poor areas from prenatal to adult life
- Parent education through social service agencies for pregnant and new parents
- Programs for fathers on their role in families and in success in schools

The federal government's efforts to reduce poverty, improve child nutrition, provide quality preschool services to impoverished parents, engage in community parent education and support, and other services for those without means should be greatly expanded. In essence, if you want severely disadvantaged children to succeed in school, they need changes in their environments, context at home, and their health. Those initiatives coupled with an imaginative school environment can produce results. We also must realize that nourishing talent takes time as children learn and develop at different rates.

FOUNDATION SIX: ACCOUNTABILITY DONE RIGHT IS IMPORTANT

Accountability for professionals in all areas of their lives is very important. Using short-term tests for any kind of serious evaluation, rather than comprehensive information, is shortsighted. Children, particularly those coming from impoverished backgrounds, do not necessarily make progress immediately or in a short period of time. Life is not the movies! One intervention doesn't produce miracles.

The impact of a teacher working with a child takes time and is more complex than what can be measured by a standardized test. Children come to school with emotional, physical, intellectual, and social needs. If any one or several of them are out of sync they affect cognitive performance and social and emotional development.

Therefore, holding teachers accountable for outcomes when many of the factors are beyond their control does not make sense. It is malpractice and wrong on the part of school boards, superintendents, and principals to hold teachers accountable for results when they do not control the variables that go into getting those results.

At a time when we all want high-quality education, politicians and bureaucrats are chasing simplistic and untested answers to improve teaching and learning. States are "racing ahead based on promises made to Washington or local political imperatives that prioritize an unwavering commitment to unproven approaches," stated Grover J. Whitehurst,[13] a senior fellow at the Brookings Institution about teacher evaluation in a *New York Times* piece on the "quirks" in states' plans.

These "quirks" raise the important issue that qualitative and quantitative data must be used properly and ethically. Data must be valid and reliable and must be analyzed properly. In addition it must be presented in understandable and clear terms, without cherry picking, misleading charts and graphs, or other questionable ways. Depending on how data is presented and how comprehensive it is, one can draw a very incomplete and often misleading conclusion, as we discussed in chapter 5.

On the surface, it seems simple. Test children to see if teachers are effective. But there are questions you have to ask about this initiative.

- Are the tests valid and reliable measures of student achievement?
- In analyzing the scores, who is included? Are students who were not in the class for the entire time period included in the data? What about special education students?
- What about transients? Some teachers face a continually changing student class load throughout the year. Are teachers responsible for the achievement level of students who did not participate in the entire process?
- What about teachers whose areas are not specifically tested—fine arts, physical education, foreign language, or social studies? How will they be assessed?
- Is it proper to evaluate teachers based on an achievement test outside their area of practice? And not even on their students but on the school-wide average?
- Does the culture and climate of the entire school affect the classroom, instruction, and achievement?
- What about the research on "value-added" analyses of performance? Are these procedures sound, ethical, reliable, valid?
- What about the role of principals and superintendents? Are they entirely culpable for the lack of student achievement based on test metrics? What should they be judged on? Leading a complex organization is much more than what is measured on achievement tests.
- How should a school be judged? On what outcomes?

Teaching is not simply implementing a recipe. It is not just engineering, "doing," and implementing. Teaching is more complex than that. It has to do with relationships and teachers and students "being" together in a caring, creative and stimulating environment.

Simplistic reliance on tests coupled with complicated rubrics can have devastating impacts. Who would want to work in a profession where you are held accountable for factors out of your control? Are creative and innovative people going to enter a profession that is perceived to be a technocratic activity, rather than a professional obligation? These are important questions. Politicians and pundits should try to teach for a week and experience the essence of teaching in a complex context with many "uncontrollables" that affect learning outcomes.

We recommend an evaluation process that ensures that the system is true to its values and beliefs and that teachers and other educators are operating ethically. This also means that not everything can be measured through metrical processes. How does one measure commitment on the part of students? Can teachers really evaluate students' emotional or social progress through tests? Teaching is much more intricate than simply a mental cognitive exercise.

Both qualitative and quantitative data are essential in determining the progress of students. Data-based decision making includes not only metrical data, but also qualitative and observational information. Teachers should be using these data, as do physicians, psychologists, psychiatrists, and others in determining progress intellectually, socially, and emotionally.

Teachers do not work in isolation of each other or the administration of the school. In that regard, all educators must work together to produce a quality school culture and climate for learning. Consequently, a comprehensive evaluation of the school should be completed and reviewed by the entire faculty and staff.

School evaluation is important and useful if educators work collaboratively together. A poor, disruptive climate effects all instruction and outcomes. To address an issue of this magnitude requires evaluating the entire school, not simply individual classrooms. A school evaluation should include "School Summits" to determine whether the school has credibility and integrity. Every two to three years the district should hold an educational summit of a cross-section of the community to review quantitative and qualitative data about whether the school's program performance and relationships match its values, principles, and plans.

Teacher evaluation should take the form of evaluations in other professions. All teachers should be held accountable for the ethical and attentive treatment of children. Teachers should have to meet a "standard of care" for the children in their classrooms and all those with whom they interact in school. The evaluation should also include their training and continued education and licensing.

Professional practice for doctors or lawyers requires meeting and maintaining certain standards. For physicians it is meeting a "standard of care." Standard of care is defined as the "ethical or legal duty of a professional to exercise the level of care, diligence, and skill prescribed in the code of practice of his or her profession, or as other professionals in the same discipline would in the same or similar circumstances."[14] If the standard of care is not met, then the teacher is negligent, improvement is then directed and, if not achieved, disciplinary action or dismissal can be taken.

An assessment based on a "standard core" should answer the following questions:

- Did the educator respond effectively to the challenges, issues, and questions confronting them?
- Can the methods/tactics implemented be supported ethically by valid research?
- Does the individual keep abreast of relevant research and obtain training in appropriate practice?
- Does the educator modify practice ethically to meet the needs of individual students?
- Are strategies and approaches modified ethically on the basis of valid data and information?

SUMMARY

Schools are about the promise of living. They are not about organizational structures, power, procedures, or management. They are about living, fully and completely, with the heart as well as the head, physically as well as intellectually, and intuitively as well as logically. Schools are not about materials and written curriculum. They are about relationships and interactions that form the nucleus around which learning and growth occur. As people experience diverse relationships, they learn more and more about themselves. Children do not become educated without the energy created from a deep connection with teachers, peers and others.

Yet the literature about schools gives you a different message. We have turned our schools into factories and complicated organizations. We talk of power, decisions, authority and participation, from top-down to bottom-up to both-ends-toward-the-middle. We agonize over the distribution of power and control. These are the games adults play. We are stuck in procedures and regulations and trapped in redesigning structures and policy.

Schools have become enamored with systems, focused on management, and bloated with jargon. They have become cold, impersonal, and competitive places concerned with test scores at a time when children need warm, caring, and nurturing environments. We are reengineering, restructuring, or reprogramming schools as if children are not a part of them. In the process, we have forgotten the nature of childhood and the process of growing up, complete with its joys and travails.

Instead, we should be giving thanks for our children. They all come to school with hope and love. They are full of anticipation and joy about learning and growing into adults. The curiosity and magic of a kindergarten classroom is testament to the natural excitement and energy children bring to school. It's natural, it's innocent and it's genuine. Fostering and building on those qualities, not destroying them through impersonal, mechanistic and factory-like environments, make schools special places that celebrate the unique destiny each child brings to this world.

Schools ought to be places where people have their heads in the clouds, not buried in the systems or policy manuals. Ideals drive schools, not procedures or regulations. Ideals are hard to define and reach because they float high in the sky beyond our fingertips, but always offering the allure of greatness. Some reformers, on the other hand, wring the idealism and the serendipity out of schools. They want everything spelled out, all contingencies covered, and instantaneous measurable results. Schools are not about trivial, pragmatic outcomes: they must pursue profound and noble goals. They are serious places of learning with excitement and creativity, and the successes and failures that come with striving. Great teachers fuse poetry with purpose and imagination with reality. To get imaginative schools, we need to change how we perceive them.

In schools with a sense of their soul and virtue, educators and parents see with new eyes. They create sanctuaries that have the whole child as the center of the experience. They develop a sense of community around educating children, and they develop an ongoing dialogue about the discrepancy between "what is" and "what can be." The focal point is long-term care for the children. In these environments, children are appreciated for their uniqueness. There is an unwavering commitment to respecting each child and the talents they possess, and to ensuring the success and development of each.

We must remember that we do not educate children for today. We educate them so they can adapt and thrive in a future with challenges we cannot define today. To do so, they need the principles, character, values, and cultural understanding that allow them to live with purpose and meaning and sustain our national principles and way of life. And, very importantly, public education has been the engine of democracy because it has been and should be free, public, and locally controlled.

NOTES

1. Robert Sternberg, "Teaching for Wisdom in Our Schools," Center for Development and Learning, www.cdl.org/resource-library/articles/teaching-wisdom.php

2. Ari deGues, *The Living Company* (Boston: Harvard Business Review Press, 2002), 1–2.

3. Mortimer Adler, *The Paideia Proposal* (New York: MacMillan, 1982), 23.

4. William Isaacs, *Dialogue: The Art of Thinking Together* (New York: Currency, 1999).

5. Joseph H. Raelin, *The Clash of Cultures* (Boston: Harvard Business Review Press, 1986), 9.

6. George A. Goens and Sharon I. R. Clover, *Mastering School Reform*, Boston: Allyn and Bacon, 1991, 177.

7. Ronald G. Corwin, "Professional Persons in Public Organizations," *Educational Administration Quarterly* 1 (Autumn 1965): 1–22.

8. Goens and Clover, *Mastering School Reform*, 167–95.

9. Peter Senge, *The Fifth Discipline* (New York: Doubleday, 2006).

10. Barry Sugarman, "Twenty Years of Organizational Learning and Ethics at Hanover Insurance: Interviews with Bill O'Brien," *Reflections* 3, no. 1.

11. Elizabeth A. City, Richard F. Elmore, Sarah E. Fiarman, and Lee Teitel, *Instructional Rounds in Education* (Cambridge, MA: Harvard Education Press, 2009).

12. Richard Rothstein, "Joel Klein's Misleading Autobiography, *American Prospect*, October 11, 2011, 42.

13. Jenny Anderson, "States Try to Fix Quirks in Teacher Evaluations," *New York Times*, February 19, 2012.

14. "Professional Standard of Care definition," BusinessDictionary.com, www.businessdictionary.com/definition/professional-standard-of-care.html#ixzz2DZAS61oy.

Chapter Ten

Eight Rules to Guide Real Reform of American Public Education

We have titled this book "*Straitjacket: How Overregulation Stifles Creativity and Innovation in Education*" because our experience tells us that regulatory control of schools has grown to such a high level that educators are fearful of trying anything new unless they are sure that student test scores will rise as a result. Public education today is mostly a top-down, fear-driven, complex organization riddled with rules and regulations that can result in a lawsuit, reprimand, or even termination if a misstep or mistake is made. As a result of control shifting to the federal level, the education of children has been constricted, curriculum has been narrowed, and instruction has been constrained by overregulation. In the final analysis we are now using narrow student achievement tests to drive much of what we do in education, including its definition, accountability, teachers' roles, and standards.

Boards of education hire superintendents to raise test scores, superintendents hire principals who can manage the enterprise and improve instruction in ways that test scores go up, and all this accountability flows down to teachers who must manage a myriad of details all focused on compliance with regulations and raising achievement on subject areas that can be tested. Even if principals and teachers have a creative idea or an innovation that they might want to try, they are constrained by a regulatory straitjacket to do so and there seems no way to break out.

As a tool for teachers, test scores are not inherently a bad thing, as these tests do measure a limited area of learning, and if the goal is to understand how well students know those learning areas, these tests can be helpful. However, the underlying psychometrics driving their construction limits what they can actually tell us about what a student knows. Focusing as we do now on these tests is not only wrong but results in a fear-driven organization where professionals become unwilling to try new approaches unless they are virtually guaranteed that test scores will improve.

Education is a victim of the "what gets measured, gets done" mentality that, in this case, has distorted the educational experience, narrowed programs to what is easily measured, and totally ignores the fact that some students require more time to learn. We are also forgetting about students' needs to identify and develop their own talents, confidence, and character that lead to success. From our point of view the issues of character, principle, values, and their wise application are absent in the test movement directed through federal reforms.

This is not the way to solve big problems. Local boards of education could do a lot to minimize this fear by broadening local accountability plans to include a host of other variables even if the state plans are test-driven. And local boards should push back at the state when entire schools are being measured by a single reading, math or writing score and teachers are being evaluated on how well their colleagues performed (such as when music, art, social studies, and science teachers are evaluated based on a school-wide average on the reading test!). Further, local boards must seriously consider the impact that the preparation gap has on all of these outcomes and provide schools and teachers the resources they need to address the lack of experience and preparation of entering students.

With regard to achievement test scores we have also argued in this book that American education is not totally broken, that in fact, much of it works well if we use tests as a measure of success. We see evidence of this in our own experiences along with national polling where many parents report that they like and approve of their local schools, the Nation's Report Card that shows the clear relationship between achievement and the preparation gap, and very recent analysis of the international tests by Stanford researchers demonstrating that American schools do well by comparison when we factor out poverty.[1] But we have also acknowledged that there are areas in need of improvement. We further believe that even where schools already perform well, they could do better if their decision-making corridor was widened and they regained more control over their working environments.

At the root cause of poor achievement lies poverty, with the resulting preparation gap that evolves from lack of opportunity. We know that poverty itself is a very tough issue to solve but we can address the preparation gap by providing these students with more time in school and with more services prior to and during their formal school years.

To distill the messages of this book we have identified eight rules to guide the further reform of American public education. It is our firm belief that if these rules were followed, more schools would do well, educators would feel reaffirmed in their roles, motivation and morale would improve, and the entire enterprise would be lifted resulting in more students learning what they truly need to know for this new century.

As we approach this last chapter we are reminded of Elliot Eisner, the Stanford professor of art and education, now emeritus, who asked us to think more broadly about how we define educational purposes. He coined the phrase "connoisseurship and criticism"[2] where he asked us to appreciate all that comprises the enterprise but also to ask how it can be improved. To this end, he argued against simplistic solutions and myopic focus on test scores.

So, here we go—eight rules to guide our thinking on how to improve education and to refocus reform efforts across the country.

RULE 1: SCHOOLS ARE NOT BUSINESSES! FOCUS ON WELL EDUCATING, NOT WELL SCHOOLING

Schools are not businesses, and children are not "products" that can be easily measured like a profit and loss balance sheet. While we can measure how well students learn to read and write, we also know that these tests are biased in many ways and that there is a very strong correlation between poverty and performance. Further, the areas that we can test are themselves limited due to the psychometrics of measurement and assessment. Therefore, there are a host of learning areas and issues that cannot be measured by these tests. If an organization focuses too much of its attention on "the tests" then a lot of schooling will be lost in the shuffle of regulation and scarce resources.

In Foundation One in chapter 9 we discussed the difference between being well schooled and becoming well educated. Students can pass standardized tests and "get the numbers" on a test yet not be well educated. There is an important difference between being well educated and well schooled. The great philosophical questions of life—truth, beauty, justice, liberty, equality, and goodness—cannot be assessed through a computer-scored test, nor can character and wisdom. We must move beyond skills in math and reading and not rob our children of culture, creativity, and a love for continuous learning, service, and wisdom.

Using this broader definition of purpose we argue that kids are not customers—they are our charges, our children for whom we care, and as their "parents" (in loco) we have a much larger mission than just preparing students for an achievement test. In keeping with this idea we see child development for what it is—developmental—and not a race. If we want all children to read at a certain level by a certain grade, then we will have to provide additional time and supports to make up for their developmental and preparation gap deficits.

We also need to provide kids time to be kids, to grow up in a healthy and happy environment. As Nichols and Berliner demonstrated in their book, too many kids are traumatized by these tests.[3]

Here are some recommendations for local districts/schools:

- First, local districts must define what an education should be for their children so that they can succeed and adapt to a fast-changing world. This includes content, concepts, thinking skills, creativity, character, and moral/ethical principles. Second, based on this definition of education, superintendents and teachers should diagnose the problems in their schools and collaborate to find solutions to the issues by capitalizing on developing a creative school culture that supports innovative solutions. This can all be done at the local level.
- Local staffs and community should be trained in the process of "dialogue."[4] There are many approaches and ideas about schools and education. To have people listen and understand, there must be more than a debate and name-calling. Dialogue is a means to think and reflect together. It is more than a conversation. In dialogue the intention is to develop a new understanding and understand the values, principles, and concepts underlying ideas—old or new. It is essential to engage in dialogue, particularly, when there are different viewpoints, interpretations, and philosophies.
- The school board and administration, in conjunction with the staff and community, should define the values under which the district schools should operate. They should be more than "we love kids" and define the school cultural values for outcomes, administration, instruction, and program. For example, one district listed four major values and identified descriptors. An example is: "We recognize, support and respect each staff member as an important individual. We show sensitivity and compassion toward each other. We recognize each person's talents and skills and delight in each other's contributions and successes. We welcome new ideas and support risk-taking and innovation without fear of failure. We expect high standards of behavior in our interaction with students and others."
- Work with the educational and support staff to define the ethical principles under which each individual and program should operate. These principles will be a part of the evaluation for each individual and to ensure program integrity.
- Examine the school curriculum and daily practice and ask principals to make reports on how they are "well-educating" vs. "well-schooling" in their schools. Review table 6.1 "List of Educational Outcomes." Which of these do you consider important? To what extent are your goals aligned with achieving those you deem as important outcomes? Finally, the man-

agement guru, Peter Drucker, asserted, "What gets measured, gets done." Conduct an audit to determine what you are measuring in reality and compare that with what is getting done. Are these outcomes aligned with the choices you made in reviewing table 6.1?
- Broaden district and school accountability plans to include variables that are not measured on achievement tests. Require that principals report regularly on these variables. These could include: participation at school events by students, parents and teachers; student and parental surveys of satisfaction with school climate; absenteeism and suspension data; examples of student work such as art shows, music performances, athletic achievements; etc.
- Broaden principal evaluation plans to include the variables discussed above and others that might be appropriate. Broaden teacher evaluation plans to include activities not easily measured that represent the interplay between teacher, student and curriculum that is defined as the instructional core. Pay closer attention to what students are actually doing, not only what the teacher is doing or what the curriculum says they should be doing.
- When using test results for any kind of evaluation demand that only cohort- or "group"-specific analyses of growth data are used. When possible, factor out preparation gap deficiencies to determine the real growth of all students on these tests so that preparation gap bias is removed to the fullest extent possible.
- Display and celebrate any student activity that demonstrates complex learning across a multitude of learning areas such as science projects, field experiences, art shows, musicals, etc.
- Boards need to ask: how can we resurrect the "mission drive" that promotes communication, information, and interconnections that encourages people to experiment, adapt, and find solutions? The first step in this direction is to define the purpose of education.

RULE 2: POLITICIZATION RESULTS IN DUMBING DOWN EDUCATION

In her recent book *The Death and Life of the Great American School System: How Testing and Choice Are Undermining Education*, Diane Ravitch argues that politicization resulted in a much stripped-down set of American history standards rendering them almost meaningless.[5] She also admits her mistake in promoting the No Child Left Behind law while at the U.S. Department of Education, now realizing the long-term impact of the adequate yearly progress component that has essentially narrowed the focus of much of American public education.

In addition, Ravitch is concerned about the corporatization and privatization of schools through the political process. She stated, "wealthy individuals are pouring unprecedented amounts of money into state and local school board races, often into places where they do not reside, to elect candidates intent on undermining and privatizing public schools." She opposes "corporate-style" reform and special interests that support "high-stakes testing, more school closures and "privatizing" of public schools."[6]

As practicing superintendents we too have seen how the political process often results in an oversimplification of complex educational issues and school finance. NCLB and misconceptions over funding requirements have led to a lost decade where schools have focused myopically on a very limited set of test outcomes resulting in the public losing confidence in their public schools that has impacted the ability to properly fund schools. We have seen this spiraling down of confidence grow over the past decade or more. The true story is that schools are a lot more successful than the general public has been led to believe.

All of this politicization is drawing attention away from the real challenges facing American education and which can be solved through a more thoughtful approach. We have no illusions that poverty itself is intractable, but we do know how to mitigate its impact on children—we can lessen the impact of the preparation gap by providing more instructional time before kindergarten and after for these children. Holding teachers and schools accountable politically for lack of parental involvement and preparation is wrong. But politics are keeping us from addressing this critical issue.

Recommendations for local districts/schools:

- Don't ignore research in policy making. Many of the problems we have discussed in this book emanate from policies that were ill conceived because they ignored the underlying research. Instead, they were developed and passed based on political ideology. When making local policy decisions, pay attention to the research and educational philosophy. Teachers and administrators must make the case for adoption of programs and ideas based on sound research.
- Local boards of education should resist the temptation of federal and state cash for policies and requirements that are onerous and in some cases, without scientific merit. We recognize how difficult this is to do in reality, especially when resources are so tight, but the alternative is worse in our judgment. By playing to these irrational requirements, especially when it refers to teacher evaluation, the heart and soul of the enterprise is at stake. Superintendents too need to speak out on this topic of politicization. Only

they have the bully pulpit to break out of this straitjacket of a "dash for the cash" because they can explain at all levels the real impact on students and teachers in their schools. Going along to get along no longer suffices. We have seen too many superintendents clam up for fear of speaking out against the state or even the federal government. We have seen too many superintendents sit back at their local board without taking a stand as the "educational advisor" about what is right and wrong about certain policies. Along with being stewards of their organizations, superintendents need to be protectors, and that means being courageous at times. Toward this end, boards and superintendents need to become activist protagonists when it comes to state and federal mandates and restrictions. They should actively testify at state legislative hearings and be in regular contact with their congressmen and women on educational issues.

- Local boards and superintendents need to tell a better story about all that is right about their schools and the true costs of running them. They should not be shy about the cost of ever-growing mandates and requirements. And they need to speak out about school finance needs at the state level, not just locally. More boards, superintendents, and mayors should jointly testify at state legislative budgetary and education hearings becoming a voice for reason and for their teachers', students', and principals' well-being and success.
- Superintendents must "make the case"—pros and cons based on the research base—to the public and school board for any reform proposals at the national or state so the public understands the positive and negative potential of those reforms and possible unanticipated consequences that bureaucrats may not understand. Staying silent in this new political context is not an option any more.
- Redefine the teacher evaluation process based on a professional model that includes teachers providing their colleagues' feedback. The professional model should include establishing a "standard of care" and ethical conduct based on this concept.
- Hold "Educational Summits" every two years in which the board listens to a cross section of community, staff, and others about how the district operates and remains true to its integrity, values, goals, outcomes, and performance. The board's role is simply to *listen*, ask clarifying questions of the participants, and solicit suggestions for improvement. The board does not make presentations or engage in debate. The administration's role is to provide information, explain data, and answer questions. After the Summit the board enters a period of reflection before setting new goals and performance outcomes.

RULE 3: ON ACHIEVEMENT AND POVERTY, FOCUS ON THE PREPARATION GAP

There is an achievement gap in this country particularly between rich and poor children, a fact that is indisputable as noted in chapter 5, and we also know that there are some schools that are dysfunctional. However, for the vast majority of schools that have an achievement gap, it is a result of the preparation gap with which students enter school. These preparation gaps are real and significant and require more time before school, after school and in school to catch up.

In the final analysis, while we cannot eliminate poverty, we can impact the preparation gap by extending time in school, after school, before school, on Saturdays, and during the summer. When possible we should extend the school year. And before children enter kindergarten we can ensure that they have a quality preschool experience that properly prepares them for formal schooling.

The answer to the preparation gap can be stated in one word—"time." These kids need more time learning the basics. When they have this time we will solve the achievement gap challenge. We need to stop denigrating our public schools, attacking teachers, and evaluating them with student achievement tests that amount to malpractice. We need to focus on the real issue—increasing instructional time year-round for these students who enter school three years behind. We know that if a student is not reading well by the end of third grade their chances for success become diminished, so all possible efforts should go into addressing these learning gaps early on in a student's education.

Recommendations for local districts/schools:

- Focus resources and energy on closing the preparation gap. Local boards of education and superintendents should redirect resources to the greatest extent possible to after school, weekend, and summer school support programs for students needing extra time to catch up on the basics of learning reading, writing, and mathematics in the early grades.
- To the extent possible superintendents should resist putting Title I resources into extra classroom teachers and support staff that work during the regular school day. Our own experiences tell us that this can lead to too many interruptions for students and staff during the regular school day. Further, using Title I to fund full-time teaching positions is exceedingly expensive and those dollars should go into after-school and Saturday programs and summer school programs instead. Doing so up to third grade would be a much more efficient use of those dollars or even scarce local dollars.

- When local funding is limited, which is often the case, school boards and superintendents should seriously consider raising class sizes in grades 4 and above and using those dollars to fund the added time program for preparation gap students in kindergarten through grade 3.
- Local boards of education should receive regular reports on how well students are doing who are behind. This should include a host of variables as noted in an earlier section and not just on achievement test scores. How often they attend school, what after-school programs/activities they participate in, how involved their parents are and what efforts are going into expanding their involvement should be part of the board reports.
- Parental training is needed from prenatal through high school. Proper prenatal nutrition and health care are crucial for a healthy child both physically and cognitively. Parents need to learn how to guide their children through early toddler development as well as how important it is that they attend to their children and read to them regularly. Further engagement is needed through the turbulent early/mid teen years and then in preparation for post high school planning. Parents cannot disengage just because their kids are getting older.
- Local schools should develop partnerships with parent organizations, hospital, clinics, social services, community colleges and universities to address parenting needs and early childhood education issues. Local creative efforts can provide a template for others who succeed.
- Find funding for four-year-old kindergarten classes taught by certificated teachers who understand child development and preparation and refinement of skills and attitudes necessary for academic success.
- Conduct a preparation gap analysis of your own district students in grades K–3. How many of them enter with a preparation gap and how large is that gap by the end of grade 3? To do this analysis, desegregate available achievement data across economic lines. Similarly, conduct a mobility analysis in all elementary grades. For each school, how many students are there at the end of the year that began school in the beginning of the year? If possible, chart these changes by month. Consider what additional resources teachers may need in schools with high mobility rates.

RULE 4: ON ORGANIZATIONS AND GOVERNANCE—LESS IS MORE!

We pointed out in earlier chapters how complex school governance and organizational structures have become over the past thirty years. That change in complexity led to the title of this book *Straitjacket: How Overregulation*

Stifles Creativity and Innovation in Education. As the rules and regulations became more and more complicated they became intertwined and there were multiple unintended consequences, thus, educators now feel as though they are caught in a regulatory straitjacket unable to spend time creating innovative solutions to daily instructional problems. We have observed firsthand the result of this loss of local control—teachers and principals became more worried about complying with an avalanche of rules and regulations than focusing on how to be more creative and innovative in problem solving.

In successful businesses and industries, fields the pundits would like to compare education to, the trend over the past twenty years has been to flatten the organization; enable distributive leadership; invest in employee training and knowledge; and encourage risk taking, creativity, and innovation. However, in educational governance, we have built in so many levels of statutory and regulatory control that local educators often feel more like whipping posts.

What would happen if we rolled back all laws impacting public education to 1999—before No Child Left Behind? Would we be better or worse off? Of course that is just not possible, but we should try to repeal or eliminate as many mandates as possible to free up school organizations. If schools are "so bad" as some pundits argue, will more regulatory control improve them? We don't think so. Instead, like in successful businesses that thrive on creativity and innovation, conditions need to be created where local educators are free to experiment and where principals have more say in how their schools are run.

Finally, the root cause of our current situation has more to do with our box-score culture than anything else. Americans love to measure things, to boil down complex issues to their most simplistic indices. Education won't thrive that way; instead, we need to broadly define what an education is, that it is about child development, moral compass, American compassion, science, the arts both visual and performance, and yes—it is also about the Three R's. But since it is too expensive to measure all of these things on an achievement test, we measure what we can, which is limited mostly to reading, writing, and mathematics.

We need to simplify our overly complex school organizations and governance structures. We need to flatten our deeply complex leadership structures as Tom Peters urged businesses to do a couple decades ago. When we do these things, teacher and principal creativity and innovation will be unleashed. But until we do, the decision-making corridor for these folks will become narrower and narrower.

Implications for local districts/schools:

- Give schools, teachers, and principals wider autonomy for running their schools but make them accountable for a wide array of student performance

measures along with parent and staff satisfaction issues. Monitor progress regularly—quarterly, not just end of year.
- Too many initiatives are confounding and spread resources too thinly—focus on a few that are really important and stay with them until implemented and successful. District goals should be long-term with objectives defined each year to demonstrate quantitative and qualitative progress.
- Although viewed as a cliché, boards of education should do their best to focus on policy issues and leave the administrating to professionals. Boards play a crucial oversight role and should shelter schools from needless political influence and meddling by single-issue constituents or even fellow board members. A simple way to get boards out of the weeds is to have them meet once a month at most, perhaps once a quarter, ideally. They should revise their local policies to allow the superintendent to operate the district as their CEO, leaving policy issues to the quarterly board meetings.
- Wherever possible attempt to lessen the levels of bureaucracy between schools and the board. In other words, boards and superintendents should try to flatten the organization as much as possible. Central administration staff is necessary to deal with the avalanche of regulation from federal and state bureaucracies, but these should be "staff-level" positions that do not require reporting up or through them by schools. The problem with "line level" positions that have reporting requirements up and down within the organization is that they tend to create more rules, regulations, and paperwork to justify their existence and to shelter themselves from responsibility. To the extent possible, principals should have regular access to their superintendents and through them, to their boards.
- Local boards of education need to adopt policies that shelter schools from political controversy as much as possible. For example, when President Obama first took office in 2009 he wanted to speak to all schoolchildren throughout the county on their need to attend to schoolwork for success. However this effort erupted in a political furor as some saw this as indoctrination! The political right, in particular, assailed local boards and superintendents demanding that the president's speech not be shown. Many school districts then adopted policies shielding principals and teachers from this sort of outside political influence putting the decision to air such broadcasts and reactions to similar issues in the hands of the faculty, where it belongs.
- In chapter 6 we discussed that the antidote to complicatedness and over-regulation should include: simplicity, new thinking and perspectives, redesign, and concern over side effects. When considering a new policy or procedure, to what extent does it encourage these attributes? What are the unintended side effects?

- Review table 4.1 and appendix B; determine your own local costs for federal and state regulations. Then decide if your board of education and superintendent could better use these funds for either the preparation gap and/or for the arts.
- School board elections should be nonpartisan, separate and apart from the partisan political process.
- State superintendents or state education commissioners should not be appointed by governors but through a statewide election. In doing so, this position would then have the ability to be an independent child advocate, not a partisan political instrument.

RULE 5: DESIGN A NEW ACCOUNTABILITY PROGRAM

Accountability has been seriously misunderstood and misapplied throughout the nation's schools in the past several decades. An accountability system based largely on student achievement test results misses the mark because the inferences that can be drawn from these tests do not include the evaluation of teachers or even schools themselves. That may be a hard reality to face, but it is the truth, as noted by several important voices including the National Academies of Science, in their report on high-stakes testing,[7] and notable researchers and psychometricians such as James Popham and Diane Ravitch. To this end we need to expand our notion of what defines school success beyond simple student achievement test scores and then build accountability and evaluation systems around all of those variables.

Schools should be using tests that provide for measuring student growth and gains over time and not those that just provide a snapshot that is not readily comparable looking back and forward in time. It is only logical and appropriate to determine how well a defined cohort of students is learning to read, for example, by measuring their learning from fall to winter to spring each year and then to follow that up again the next year and the next and so on. If the tests were designed to allow for such achievement growth analysis, then we could much more accurately determine how well they are learning to read. Unfortunately, many are not so designed.

We need to greatly expand our notion of accountability to include the softer side of educational experiences and to provide a balanced report of all important indicators not just of a few test score areas where is it relatively easy and inexpensive to measure.

Recommendations for local districts/schools:

- Boards of education and superintendents should invest in the assessment literacy of their principals and teachers. If more educators better understood testing issues we would not be in the mess we find ourselves.

- Superintendents, as busy as they are, need to take on a leadership role about the fair and proper use of tests. They need to become assessment literate themselves and lead the way on the proper design and interpretation of fair accountability systems.
- James Popham's 2001 book *The Truth about Testing: An Educator's Call to Action* is a classic.[8] Buy a copy for all your administrators and hold discussions about its relevance and impact. Learn about the proper uses of tests along with the improper uses. Balance state achievement tests with more regular formative assessments. Implement assessments that are strongly related to curriculum mastery, not spreading out and discriminating among students, and use only those assessments where annual growth for students and matched cohorts can be properly calculated. Learn about the perils of high-stakes testing.
- Conduct an audit of all the tests students take, especially in the elementary schools. How much time do they take from instruction? To what extent do teachers actually use the results in modifying instruction (do this anonymously to get a true picture)? Determine the mix of formative vs. summative assessments—work to emphasize use of formative over summative assessments.
- Boards and superintendents should recognize that the more they focus on achievement test results the more teachers and principals will focus on them too. This can lead to too much test prep and even cheating by teachers and principals worried about job security over variables they otherwise have little control over. The mantra "what gets measured gets done" should guide board discussions, policies, and accountability plans. If boards start focusing on school measures that are not related to tests, schools will begin paying more attention to those broader outcomes.
- Conduct your own parental poll following the design of the annual PDK poll on parent satisfaction. Be sure to ask parents how they feel about state standardized tests.
- Conduct a poll of teachers and ask them how much they use *state standardized tests* to drive instruction.
- Analyze student achievement by matched cohort over time to determine growth. There are many ways to crunch achievement data so that cohort results are identified. These results should be the core of test-driven accountability plans but then only in conjunction with other variables as discussed above in earlier sections. If your assessment system does not permit such analyses due to construction limitations, change the assessment program.
- Do not evaluate teachers in whole or even in part using student achievement tests. We have discussed the reasons why this is a bad idea. Think of it this way: how would you feel if your job evaluation and security depended on how employees did in a department other than yours, on measures that

have nothing to do with your job, and on an instrument that had limited value to measure the overall health and progress of the enterprise?
- Teacher assessment should be revised around a professional model to include whether the teacher meets a "standard of care" for their students and operates in accord with defined professional ethics, and should include a review of their performance by peers as well as principals and administrators. The same approach should be taken with principals.
- Master union contracts should concern salary and fringe benefits, but exclude issues relating to determining curricular program or operational policy. Master contracts can also straitjacket reform and innovation. This would provide teachers protection in compensation, as well as their liberty and property rights.

RULE 6: LIMIT THE ROLE OF THE U.S. DEPARTMENT OF EDUCATION

Underlying our recommendations is the belief that the states and localities should maintain the locus of control for public education. Quality education for children requires a partnership between parents and educators working together for the educational welfare of children. This cannot happen from a "one-size-fits-all" approach from Washington. Highly regulated approaches like No Child Left Behind and Race to the Top do not and have not worked. The federal record over the past thirty years has been one of failure complete with red tape, bureaucracy, and constraints on local schools. The coercive approach to federal reform efforts does not produce commitment or attract talent to our schools. In fact it does the opposite. In addition, responsibility for education rests constitutionally with states—not with the federal government.

Altering, limiting, or eliminating any federal department is a herculean and daunting task. Bureaucracy, once established, has a self-perpetuating quality. But in light of the Constitution and the continued failure of federal efforts we think it is time to return educational responsibility to the states and localities, not just in lip service but also in practice.

Creativity is born through local energy and insight to find solutions. Does anyone really think the solution to our children's education rests in Washington? The federal government can help local educators and states through research grants. In this way, the federal department can promote local innovation and creative solutions.

Creativity and innovation cannot be mandated from Washington, D.C., or even at the state or district level—it is accomplished at the school and teacher level every day. As we have stated throughout this book, federally mandated "school reform" has failed because it has focused on the wrong things. And it has failed largely because it was a top-down approach. Organizational science tells us that top-down improvement initiatives rarely succeed, and education is no different.

School improvement is accomplished at the classroom level. It is practiced within the instructional core, where dynamic teachers experiment with interesting and challenging curricula, engaging students to enhance their motivation, self-regulation, and thus their own learning. This level of work does not lend itself to universal solutions dictated from either the federal or state levels.

As a result of the many federal failures that have misguided the public, often leading to a loss of confidence in their public schools, we argue that the U.S. Department of Education should either be eliminated or, at the least, its mission should be seriously curtailed. If not eliminated altogether, which we advocate for, its mission should be narrowed to those existing programmatic successes that impact the preparation gap and civil rights, such as Title I, Title II, Title IX, and IDEA (but the level of funding for IDEA/special education needs to be increased significantly so that regular education programming is not disadvantaged as a result of paying for special education).

Recommendations for local districts/schools:

- Boards of education and superintendents should examine for themselves what positive role the U.S. Department of Education has for their districts and schools. In those deliberations consider that all federal funding would be sent to the district as a block grant. Further, funding for IDEA—special education—should be increased to better match the actual costs of complying with these expensive mandates. If they come to the same conclusion as we have, then they should lobby their state associations and congressmen/women to make changes at the federal level.
- If not eliminated, reduce the role of the federal Department of Education to funding research and development projects at the local level, providing total financial support for federally adopted programs, for example, special education, Title I, and others. Be a clearinghouse of successful innovative programs developed at the local level for other states.

RULE 7: NOT ALL SCHOOLS ARE FAILING—STOP DENIGRATING AMERICAN PUBLIC EDUCATION

Most schools in the United States are doing very well—contrary to popular opinion. The facts from the Nation's Report Card (National Assessment of Educational Progress or NAEP test) as presented in chapter 5 clearly demonstrate that schools without high concentrations of poor and disadvantaged students are performing well on this rigorous test. NAEP also shows the strong relationship between the preparation gap and the achievement gap. Therefore, if we want to improve achievement in all schools we need to more directly address poverty and other indices of the disadvantaged.

Much is also often made of how poorly American students do compared to their international peers. A recent study from Stanford University and the Economic Policy Institute points out that this is just not true. Martin Carnoy and Richard Rothstein, in their report "What Do International Tests Really Show about U.S. Student Performance?" demonstrate that American students do just as well as others around the world on the Program on International Student Assessment (PISA), Trends in International Mathematics and Science Study (TIMSS), and two forms of the domestic National Assessment of Educational Progress (NAEP).

The bottom line is that American schools are not performing as poorly as commonly believed. We should have more confidence in our schools and we should stop denigrating them. Instead, we should be more fully supporting them for the difficult challenges they face in closing the preparation gap with which so many kids enter school.

Recommendations for local districts/schools:

- Interpreting national, state, and local test results is complex and requires a good deal of assessment knowledge. Boards and superintendents should take the time to hear from experts on how to interpret international, national, state mastery, and local tests so as to form a proper and balanced view of how well students are truly performing.
- Local districts should provide in-service for all professional staff in data, data management, and data analysis. Principals and teachers should be able to interpret data for parents and present them in ethical and clear ways.
- Both qualitative and quantitative data and assessments should be analyzed across cohorts of students and parents longitudinally, not just on a short-term basis.
- Local boards and superintendents should promote the positive achievement of students at every opportunity and to broaden their definition of success. As the steward of the schools and the voice of students, they should promote public education for all the good that it has done and should do going forward.

RULE 8: A CREATIVE ORGANIZATIONAL CULTURE WILL ATTRACT TALENTED AND INNOVATIVE PEOPLE AND ENCOURAGE, NOT SUPPRESS THEIR CREATIVITY

What do Google, Wegmans Food Markets, Edward Jones, Recreational Equipment, Chesapeake Energy, USAA, Qualcomm, Whole Foods Markets,

Baptist Health South Florida, and Intel all have in common? They are the top ten companies to work for rated by size by *Fortune*.

What do Salesforce.com, Alexion, Amazon.com, Red Hat, Intuitive Surgical, Edwards Lifesciences, FMC Technologies, Cerner, Monsanto, and Perrigo all have in common? They are the top ten most innovative companies as rated by *Forbes*.

But at the center of all of these corporate successes are the people they attract, employ, and retain. To be the top companies to work for or the top innovative companies, they need creative and innovative employees to drive that innovation.

The reason why these companies are so successful is not only competition, it is because they have created a culture and organization that promotes and encourages creativity and innovation, which attracts the best and brightest. Further, these employees are given the space to experiment and exercise their creativity in teams to develop innovative solutions to tough problems.

School cultures and organizations, on the other hand, have become restrictive, regulatory, and compliance-driven. Principals and teachers work in a "gotcha" environment where the slightest mistake can bring public criticism, blog posts that denigrate individuals, lawsuits, and even termination with the most recent advent of student achievement test–driven teacher and principal evaluation systems. And to make things worse, the measures on which we evaluate schools is a very narrow set of outcomes. Schooling is so much more than a math or reading test.

Ask yourself: where would you want to work? Where would you want your kids to work? Where do you think they would be most engaged, successful and happy: in one of the most innovative companies to work for or in an American public school?

We believe that to free up teacher and principal creativity and innovation, schools need to widen their corridor for decision making and we need to lessen the top-down control and regulation within which they work. The bottom line is that teachers and principals need to be freed from the straitjacket of centralized control and regulation and work in a less restrictive work environment. They need to experiment without fear of retribution should their work not succeed the first time out. They need to have more control over what they do each hour, each day, and each month. None of the companies listed above would be successful if their rules and regulations drove out their talent and best and brightest.

Recommendations for local districts/schools:

- Local boards and superintendents would do well to survey their professional staff via anonymous methods to determine how constrained they feel about their work. To the extent possible locally, work to diminish the

constraints and free up teachers, teacher teams and principals to be more innovative when developing programs.
- With so much time, energy, and resources going into personnel recruitment, an added dimension should be included—the degree to which prospective employees have demonstrated creative and innovative solutions to tough instructional problems.
- Local boards and superintendents should ask themselves—do they honor, acknowledge, and reward creativity or do their policies and practices serve to actually suppress such innovation? What is rewarded and what is sanctioned both explicitly and implicitly?
- Who do principals report to and for what? Answering this question would go a long way toward freeing up the organization and making it safer for otherwise creative teachers and principals to innovate. Principals need access to their superintendents and should be heard at the board level.
- Superintendents are more than program and fiscal managers. Evaluating superintendents should include qualitative and quantitative information and ethical and legal responsibilities, but also the creation of a system that values and nourishes its talent through professional challenges and a sense of efficacy through and imaginative and creative work culture.
- Review the sections of chapter 5 on "Teachers, Evaluation, and Tests"; "Evaluating Teachers and Validity and Reliability"; and "Junk Science." Conduct a board discussion on the merits of this discussion. Hire a local professor from a nearby college or university knowledgeable about tests and measurement if necessary to act as moderator. After this discussion if you agree with us on this issue, do everything you can to mitigate the impacts of these policies on your teachers by strengthening the other components of the evaluation system to minimize the impact of using test scores. *Teachers are your greatest resource and they deserve such consideration.*

EPILOGUE

> In teaching you cannot see the fruit of a day's work. It is invisible and remains so, maybe for 20 years.
>
> —Jacques Barzun

Did teachers have an impact on your life? Most people can identify a teacher or teachers who helped make them what they are today. Many of our lives would not be as rich and full without the fair-minded guidance, patience, discipline, or caring and nurturing of a teacher. Their sage advice rings in our ears for decades and supports and reinforces us in easy as well as difficult times.

The significance of teachers may not be felt for years. The relationship between student and teacher cannot always be easily assessed, and may not demonstrate itself in multiple-choice tests. It goes far beyond performance on metrical "data" and assessments. Tests fade into obscurity but the intangibles of a significant relationship with a teacher live on forever. They are the bonds and times we recall when we reflect on who we are and how we got here.

Children have to work through the developmental stages of growth, face the socioeconomic realities of their families, try to find their place in the world, and confront their insecurities and uncertainties. Teachers are critical anchors that help them, support them, and provide direction.

Teaching is not a robotic act of engineering—it is much more complicated. The genuine human connection between two people cannot be manufactured simply by following a formula or process. It rests in the energy, empathy, compassion, patience, and passion that allow students to invest in teachers' care, knowledge, and guidance. That relationship is unique. One teacher may be significant to one child, but may not have the same affect on others because children differ and significant relationships are very individualized.

We all know children who didn't do well on tests or other academic measures because of their developmental, social, and emotional needs or intrinsic or extrinsic motivation. But years later, they got advanced degrees, became entrepreneurs, or found themselves as lawyers, physicians, entertainers, business owners, and teachers.

In reality, there are no quick fixes to academic achievement. Reliance on short-term assessments like standardized tests may actually do tremendous damage to children whose potential can only be unlocked over time. Children are not receptacles of facts and figures. They are individuals with potential and talent that become tangible because of the genuine relationship with a teacher and the intangible connection between them.

As Einstein said, "it is the supreme art of the teacher to awaken joy in creative expression and knowledge." The art of teaching involves creating a relationship with students that inspires students to not settle for anything but their best, recognizes that talent and creativity take time to develop, provides compassionate and patient support, and creates a caring, demanding, and safe environment to try, fail, and succeed. The art of teaching cannot be measured simplistically. It actually sets the stage for the successful application of the science of teaching.

The awakening of motivation, creativity and expression may not take place for years. But without that significant relationship with the teacher, it may not take place at all. Teachers celebrate life by helping children face their yearning for belonging and find their calling in their pursuit and dreams of a good and happy life. That cannot be done in a straitjacket.

NOTES

1. M. Carnoy, and R. Rothstein *What Do International Tests Really Show about U.S. Student Performance?* (Washington, DC: Economic Policy Institute, 2013), www.epi.org/publication/us-student-performance-testing/

2. Elliot W. Eisner, "Educational Connoisseurship and Criticism," *Journal of Aesthetic Education* 10, nos. 3–4 (1976): 135–50.

3. Sharon Lynn Nichols, and David C. Berliner, *Collateral Damage: How High-Stakes Testing Corrupts America's Schools* (Cambridge, MA: Harvard Education Press, 2007).

4. William Isaac, *Dialogue and the Art of Thinking Together* (New York: Doubleday, 1999), 20–46.

5. Diane Ravitch, *The Death and Life of the Great American School System: How Testing and Choice Are Undermining Education* (New York: Basic Books, 2011).

6. Michelle McNeil, "Diane Ravitch Launches New Education Advocacy Counterforce," *Education Week*, March 7, 2013.

7. Jay P. Heubert and Robert M. Hauser, eds., *High Stakes: Testing for Tracking, Promotion, and Graduation* (Washington, DC: National Academies Press, 1999).

8. James Popham, W. *The Truth about Testing: An Educator's Call to Action.* Alexandria, VA: Association for Supervision and Curriculum Developments, 2001.

Appendix A

History of Federal Involvement in Education

Year/Decade	Legislation/Policy
1785	The United States valued education under the Articles of Confederation before adoption of the Constitution. In fact, the land ordinance of 1785 specified that section 16 in every township was reserved for the establishment of a public school. As the country moved west to what was to become Michigan, Wisconsin, Illinois, Ohio, Indiana, and Minnesota there was the establishment of an educational system that was local and proximate to the citizens. While the statute was national, education remained local.
	Land was to be systematically surveyed into square townships, six miles on a side. Each of these townships was subdivided into thirty-six sections of one square mile. The ordinance was significant for establishing a mechanism for establishing and funding schools because section 16 in each township was reserved for the maintenance of public schools. Local school boards were established and the concept of local control was instituted.
	In moving beyond a confederation to a union of states under the Constitution, the issue of education was left to the province of the states. There was no explicit mention of public education in the U.S. Constitution. The power to establish schools was reserved for the states. "The powers not delegated to the United States by the Constitution, nor prohibited by it to the States, are reserved to the States respectively, or to the people."
1867	The original "office of education" at the federal level was established to "help the states to establish effective school systems," not direct or control them.
1890	The Morrill Act gave the department of education responsibility for administering support for land grant colleges and universities.
1917	Vocational education became a priority with the passage of the Hughes Act.
1941	The George-Bearden Act highlighted agricultural, industrial, and home economics training for high school youngsters.
1941-4	During World War II, the federal involvement in education increased with the Lanham Act (1941) that provided funds to local school systems to ease the fiscal burden of having the presence of military and other "installations" in local communities. The landmark G.I. Bill in 1944 authorized postsecondary education assistance to veterans.
1958	The first example of comprehensive federal education legislation was passed in 1958. Facing the Cold War, the National Defense Education Act (NDEA) was passed to respond to the Sputnik launch. Competition with the Soviet Union in science and technical fields was the motivation. The NDEA promoted science, mathematics, and foreign language education in elementary and secondary schools because of the so-called Sputnik crisis. This bill affected elementary, secondary, and college education.

1960s

Poverty and civil rights were major issues in the 1960s and 1970s and resulted in the passage of Title VI of the Civil Rights Act of 1962. A watershed year for the increased involvement of the federal government and public education was 1965 with the enactment of the "Elementary and Secondary Education Act (ESEA). This act authorized grants for elementary and secondary programs specifically geared to low-income families, library resources, textbooks, and other materials to supplement local education agencies. In addition, research and professional development were also part of this package. The key to these legislative initiatives was civil rights enforcement, which became "a fundamental and long-lasting focus of the Department of Education."

"Title" programs were also part of this period. In addition, during this period Title III funding for innovative projects was passed, with many projects focusing on open classrooms, team teaching, alternative schools, and the like. Title V provided federal aid to strengthen state education agencies and Operation Head Start was established. The focus was on ensuring that children of poverty would have their needs addressed, as well as having the federal government become involved in encouraging innovative projects. In addition, the National Assessment of Educational Progress (NAEP) was established in 1969 to carry out surveys of students' academic achievements with the results to be reported by the "nation and region, but not individual states, districts, or students."

1970s

Title IX of the Education Amendments of 1972 and Section 504 of the Rehabilitation Act of 1973 prohibiting discrimination based on race, sex, and disability. This legislation made civil rights a cornerstone of the Department of Education.
The decade of the 1970s brought landmark legislation concerning the education of handicapped children. In 1975, Congress passed Public Law 94-142 (Education of All Handicapped Children Act), now codified as IDEA (Individuals with Disabilities Education Act). In order to receive federal funds, states must develop and implement policies that assure a free appropriate public education to all children with disabilities. Public Law 94-142 mandated that each handicapped child get an individualized education in the least restrictive environment. The Supreme Court in *Lau v. Nichols* ruled that school districts must provide remedies for non-English-speaking children so they have access to education. This decade echoed the 1960s with its emphasis on children in poverty or with language as handicapping condition to have the ability to gain an education in public schools.

(continued)

Year/Decade	Legislation/Policy
1979	The establishment of the Federal Department of Education in 1979 was extremely controversial and solidified a larger role for the federal government in education. People of all political dispositions questioned its necessity. Every state in the union has a department of education and local boards of education to set and implement educational policy. Opponents of a cabinet-level educational department were concerned about the impact on "independent" local schools. Included in the debate on the Senate bill to create the department were amendments on school prayer, sex education, unionization of teachers, and affirmative action. All were defeated by roll-call votes. An amendment to create in the department an office of Bilingual Education and Minority Affairs was adopted. The Senate bill passed 72-21. The House version, H. R. 2444 was reported out of the House Governmental Operations Committee by one vote, 20-19. This version included a series of amendments on such topics as busing, racial quotas, abortion and school prayer. The House bill passed by a four-vote margin, 210-206. The two versions went to a conference committee that dropped most of the House provisions and the Senate adopted the conference report 69-22, and the House agreed with the conference report by a 215-201 margin. Looking back, the opposition was significant, particularly in the House. The nature of the amendments in the Senate and the House should give anyone pause about federal involvement in education. The politicization of education with the power of controlling education in every state and every local community should concern everyone of any political persuasion. The federal government seldom reverses itself once it creates a department or piece of legislation. Fixing legislation "later" is folly. Rescinding federal legislation is pure fantasy.
1983	In 1983 *A Nation at Risk: The Imperative for Educational Reform* was a report from Ronald Reagan's National Commission on Excellence in Education and was considered a landmark event in modern American educational history, which stoked the flames of local, state, and federal reform efforts.
1985	The charter school movement started.
1994	The Educate America Act: Goals 2000. Set challenging goals for school to achieve by the year 2000.
2001	No Child Left Behind act was enacted with bipartisan support and required all students to be proficient in reading, mathematics, and science by 2014, with annual yearly progress measures to determine success, annual standardized tests in grades 3–8 in reading and mathematics, and reports by disaggregated groups of students. Sanctions on schools were included for districts not meeting AYP requirements and schools were required to develop plans to close the achievement gap. school plans to close achievement gaps.
2009	Race to the Top was created to spur innovation and reforms in state and local district K–12 education. It was funded by the American Recovery and Reinvestment Act of 2009. Included were certain educational policies, such as performance-based standards for teachers and principals, complying with nationwide standards, promoting charter schools and privatization of education, and computerization.

Appendix B

Mandates—Bristol, CT, Public Schools

Partially Funded Mandates	Estimated Funds/ Hours for 2008-2009	Hourly Rate Applied	Extended Cost
Adult Education - Bristol Share (Total: $512,000)	$308,581		$308,581
CAPT Testing - Grade 10	100+ hours per year	$ 8,300	$ 8,300
CMT Testing - Grades 4/6/8 Expanded Testing	500+/ 45 hours per year	$ 45,235	$ 45,235
Preparation for mandated science testing in grades 5/8 (2007)	60 hours	$ 4,980	$ 4,980
English Language Learners - ELL & Bilingual	$547,916		$547,916
Special Education District Share (65%)	$ 7,549,694		$7,549,694
Un-Funded Mandates			
ADA accommodations (transportation/signs/elevators)	$100,000		$100,000
Alternate Education for Expelled Students ($12,000 per student)	$33,300		$33,300
Air Quality	$4,000		$4,000
Asbestos Training for Building Grounds Staff (1 day per year)	$200		$200
Background Checks and Finger Printing (Follow-up)	$1,250		$1,250
BEST Program (Subs & Oversight)	$17,000		$17,000
Bullying Policy (investigations/record keeping/follow-up)	$7,500		$7,500
Child Abuse Reporting (200 per year @ $120 per)	$24,000		$24,000
Continuing Education Units (CEU Professional Development) 18 hours	$870,166		$870,166
CPR/First Aid and Heimlich Training (nurses/coaches/staff)	$2,000		$2,000
Hepatitis B (@ $120)	$120		$120
Drug Education (health staff)	$130,000		$130,000
ED-001 END OF YEAR SCHOOL REPORT (audit cost)	200 hours and $30,000	$ 16,600	$ 46,600
ED-014 MINIMUM EXPENDITURE COMPLIANCE CHECK	2 hours per year	$ 166	$ 166
ED-156 FALL HIRING SURVEY	2 hours per year	$ 166	$ 166
ED-163 CONNECTICUT SCHOOL DATA REPORT	64 hours per year	$ 5,312	$ 5,312
ED-166 DISCIPLINE OFFENSE REPORT	360 hours per year	$ 29,880	$ 29,880
ED-525 STUDENT DROPOUT REPORT	30 hours per year	$ 2,490	$ 2,490
ED-540 GRADUATION CLASS REPORT	30 hours per year	$ 2,490	$ 2,490
ED-006S PUBLIC SCHOOL INFORMATION (PSIS)	$35,000		$35,000

Item	Hours/Cost	Amount	Total
ED-612 LANGUAGE ASSESSMENT SCALES DATA COLLECTION	100 hours per year	$ 8,300	$ 8,300
ED-003 TEACHER/ADMINISTRATORS NEGOTIATIONS	$ 25,000		$ 25,000
ED-162 NON-CERTIFIED STAFF	8 hours per year	$ 664	$ 664
ED-607 SURVEY OF TITLE IX COORDINATORS	2 hours per year	$ 166	$ 166
ED-172 REQUEST 90 DAY CERTIFICATION	10 hours per year	$ 830	$ 830
ED-1723 REQUEST TEMPORARY AUTHORIZATION FOR MINOR A	5 hours per year	$ 415	$ 415
ED-175 SPECIAL WAIVER FOR SUBSTITUTE	4 hours per year	$ 332	$ 332
ED-177 REQUEST-DURATIONAL SHORTAGE AREA PERMIT	2 hours per year	$ 166	$ 166
ED-186 APPLICATION-TEMP/EMERGENCY COACHING PERMIT	2 hours per year	$ 166	$ 166
ED-017 GRANT APPLICATION NONPUBLIC HEALTH SERVICES	2 hours per year	$ 166	$ 166
ED-021 OUT OF TOWN MAGNET SCHOOL TRANSPORTATION	6 hours per year	$ 498	$ 498
ED-111 CASH MANAGEMENT REPORT	60 hours per year	$ 4,980	$ 4,980
ED-114 GRANT BUDGET REVISION	100 hours per year	$ 8,300	$ 8,300
ED-141 STATEMENT OF EXPENDITURES FED/STATE PROJECTS	60 hours per year	$ 4,980	$ 4,980
ED-042 REQUEST FOR REVIEW OF FINAL PLANS	100 hours per year	$ 8,300	$ 8,300
ED-042CO NOTICE OF CHANGE ORDER	20 hours per year	$ 1,660	$ 1,660
ED-046 REQUEST FOR SCHOOL CONSTRUCTION PROGRESS PAYM	20 hours per year	$ 1,660	$ 1,660
ED-049 GRANT APP FOR SCHOOL BUILDING PROJECT	100 hours per year	$ 8,300	$ 8,300
ED-050 SCHOOL FACILITIES SURVEY	2 hours per year	$ 166	$ 166
ED-053 SITE ANALYSIS	20 hours per year	$ 1,660	$ 1,660
ED-099-AGREEMENT FOR CHILD NUTRITION PROGRAMS	2 hours per year	$ 166	$ 166
ED-103 REIMBURSEMENT CLAIM NAT. SCHOOL LUNCH PROGRA	12 hours per year	$ 996	$ 996
ED-205 TITLE I EVALUATION REPORT	30 hours per year	$ 2,490	$ 2,490
SEDAC (SPECIAL EDUCATION INFORMATION SYSTEM)	2,100 hours and $ 65,000	$ 174,300	$ 239,300
ED-229 BILINGUAL EDUCATION GRANT APPLICATION	30 hours per year	$ 2,490	$ 2,490
ED-241/241A ADULT EDUCATION SUMMARY REPORT	30 hours per year	$ 2,490	$ 2,490
ED-244/244A GRANT APPLICATION FOR ADULT EDUCATION	30 hours per year	$ 2,490	$ 2,490
ED-245/245A GRANT APPLICATION REVISION-ADULT EDUCATIO	10 hours per year	$ 830	$ 830
ED-236 IMMIGRANT STUDENT SURVEY REPORT	2 hours per year	$ 166	$ 166
ED-613A STATE DISTRICT CONSOLIDATION APPLICATION	30 hours per year	$ 2,490	$ 2,490
ED-613B FEDERAL DISTRICT CONSOLIDATION APPLICATION	200 hours per year	$ 16,600	$ 16,600
Family and Medical Leave Act (@$6,000 per plus cost of sub)	$254,200		$254,200
sub-cost	$246,000		$246,000
Freedom of Information Legal Costs & Administration	$12,000		$12,000
Health Insurance Portability and Accountability Act (HIPAA)	5 hours per year	$ 415	$ 415
Internet Protection Act for Children(software and staff cost)	$9,000		$9,000
Jury Duty (50@ cost of sub)	$3,250		$3,250
Medicaid Reimbursement (OT/PT/Speech/Psy)	$60,000		$60,000
Minority Staff Recruitment	$7,000		$7,000
No Child Left Behind Act (NCLB) Report	100 hours per year	$ 8,300	$ 8,300
Paraprofessional Mandates for Title 1 Schools (highly qualified)	20 hours per year	$ 1,660	$ 1,660

McKenny-Vento Act	200 hours per year	$ 16,600	$ 16,600
AYP Reporting/action	350 hours per year	$ 29,050	$ 29,050
Military Recruitment	40 hours per year	$ 3,320	$ 3,320
Homeless Transportation (@ $150 per day for a school year, per student)	$65,000		$65,000
Data Collection	750 hours per year	$ 62,250	$ 62,250
Policy related expenses	300 hours per year	$ 24,900	$ 24,900
Non-public school transportation	$982,522		$982,522
Pesticide Applications Policy	6 hours per year	$ 498	$ 498
Promotion and Graduation Requirements	500 hours per year	$ 41,500	$ 41,500
Restraint Training for Special Education and Support Staff	$10,000		$10,000
Residency investigation	$10,000		$10,000
Restaurant Safety Act (signs)	$600		$600
School Records and Retention	$5,000		$5,000
School Transportation Safety Reporting	$5,000		$5,000
Sexual Harassment Training	$1,250.00		$1,250
Student Survey	20 hours per year	$ 1,660	$ 1,660
Special Education Due Process (proactive)	$70,000		$70,000
Special Education Excess Cost our share plus 5% state Reduction	$700,000		$700,000
Special Education Coverage at PPT's	5000 hours per year	$ 415,000	$ 415,000
Gifted and Talented	$127,722		$127,722
Strategic School Profiles (SSP) (data collection/reporting)	200 hours per year	$ 16,600	$ 16,600
Student Physicals and Immunizations (Grades K,7,10)	1000 hours per year	$ 83,000	$ 83,000
Hearing Screenings	$30,000		$30,000
School Medical Advisor	$6,000		$6,000
Related Medical Equipment	$150,000		$150,000
Summer School or other supplemental services for intervention	$86,804		$86,804
Teacher/Administrator Evaluations	$500,000		$500,000
Transportation to Regional Vo/AG/Technical Schools	$297,000		$297,000
Truancy Reporting (10 per year)	$30,000		$30,000
Tuition to Regional Vo/AG schools	$200,000		$200,000
Vending Machines	20 hours per year	$ 1,660	$ 1,660
504 Accommodations	$35,000		$35,000

TOTAL COSTS FOR MANDATES: $14,733,344

About the Authors

George A. Goens, PhD, has authored six other books, has written over sixty articles in journals and magazines on leadership and education, and has appeared on radio programs discussing leadership and organizational development. He has worked with public and private sector organizations on leadership selection, development, and assessment.

Dr. Goens has also presented seminars and workshops on leadership, school reform, and leading in a crisis at regional and state conferences and for organizations and school districts across the country. In addition, he has designed educational programs and curriculum for schools serving urban children in Milwaukee. He served as a Wisconsin superintendent of schools for fifteen years, where he was awarded the title of "Outstanding Educator." He was born in Chicago, Illinois, and earned a PhD from the University Wisconsin. He currently lives in Litchfield, Connecticut. His website is www.georgegoens.com

Philip Streifer is president and CEO of EDvisualize, LLC (www.EDvisualize.com), a consulting company focusing on school improvement through improved leadership. Most recently he was superintendent of the Bristol (CT) Public Schools, and prior to that he was associate professor of educational leadership at the University of Connecticut. He held two earlier superintendencies in suburban districts (Avon, CT, and Barrington, RI). He serves as a North West Education Association board member (NWEA.org) and a regent of the University of Hartford. He was chairperson of the Connecticut Association of Urban Superintendents and president of the Connecticut Coalition for Justice in Education Funding.

Dr. Streifer has spoken and published nationally on a range of issues focusing on school improvement. His first book, *Using Data to Make Better Edu-*

cational Decisions (Rowman & Littlefield Education, 2002) was copublished with the American Association of School Administrators. His second book addressed the current state of the art of data driven decision making. He holds a PhD in educational administration from the University of Connecticut, a master's degree from Central CT State University in school administration, and a bachelor's degree in music education from the Hartt School, The University of Hartford.

www.ingramcontent.com/pod-product-compliance
Lightning Source LLC
Chambersburg PA
CBHW061841300426
44115CB00013B/2469